CCDA THEOLOGICAL JOURNAL 2015 EDITION

EDITED BY

Mae Cannon

Soong-Chan Rah

Chanequa Walker-Barnes

Brandon Wrencher

CCDA PUBLISHING
WWW.CCDA.ORG

CCDA Theology Committee

The purpose of the CCDA Theology Committee is to articulate the theological foundations of Christian community development and to foster theological engagement within and beyond the community of CCDA.

The committee's primary work has been to produce the CCDA Theological Journal.

Chanequa Walker-Barnes—Co-Chair
Soong-Chan Rah—Co-Chair
Vince Bantu
Mae Cannon
M. Daniel Carroll R.
Dominique DuBois Gilliard
Bethany Harris
Brandon Wrencher

Contents

Letter from the Editors
CCDA Theology Committee

Part I: CCDA National Conference Theme: "Illuminate"

The Deformed Imagination of How We Are Light and What We Call Darkness
Mikael Broadway

The Light Shines in the Darkness: Some Implications of John's Theology of Light For CCDA
Joshua Beckett

Be the Light: Illumination Towards Racial Justice
Liz Mosbo-VerHage

Part II: Deepening the Ministry of CCDA

Jesus' Solidarity with the Prisoner: A Christology of Incarceration and Reentry
Eric Harmon

Ida B. Wells: Poetic Justice
Dominique DuBois Gilliard

From Ferguson to Memphis: Theological Reflections & Engaged Praxis
Andre E. Johnson

What Are All Those Women of Color Doing in That Room? Reflections From the Rainbow
Chanequa Walker-Barnes, Oluwatomisin Oredein, AnaYelsi Velasco-Sanchez, Ginny Giles, & Sandra Van Opstal

Part III: Book Reviews

Prophetic Lament: A Call for Justice in Troubled Times
M. Daniel Carroll R.

Where the Cross Meets the Street: What Happens to the Neighborhood When God is at the Center
Zakiya Jackson

Dear White Christians: For Those Still Longing for Reconciliation
Brandon Wrencher

Letter from the Editors

Welcome to the fourth annual issue of the CCDA Theological Journal. The Theological Committee of the CCDA presents this volume in conjunction with the 2015 CCDA National Conference. The 2015 theme is Illuminate. This year's journal presents articles on the conference topic as well as articles that connect us more deeply with the work of Christian Community Development.

Mikael Broadway, Associate Professor of Theology and Ethics at Shaw University Divinity School wrestles with passages of Scripture related to the notion of "light" and "darkness" and how implicit cultural or racial biases have blemished our interpretation and misinformed our theology and understanding of these notions of Biblical imagery. Joshua Beckett's essay was chosen from an open call for papers from the CCDA community. He reflects on the theme of light in the Gospel of John. Beckett addresses the nature and scope of the human dimension of "being light," the need to respond to detractors without judgment, and the invitation to cross-cultural divides. Our first section examines the national conference theme from several different perspectives. Liz Mosbo-Verhage, associate pastor at Quest Church in Seattle reflects on the meaning of "light" in Matthew 5:14-16, offering a reading that names illumination as a call to discipleship that should embody justice, racial reconciliation and transformative hope.

Our second section attempts to deepen our engagement with various topics that serve our communities. In "Jesus' Solidarity with the Prisoner: A Christology of Incarnation and Reentry," Eric Harmon, another article chosen from our open call for papers, writes about how the Biblical account of Jesus sheds light on the ways Christians and the world should view and respond to those who are imprisoned in various ways. Dominique DuBios Gilliard offers a reflection on local justice ministry in Memphis by recalling the story of Ida B. Wells. Andre Johnson of Memphis Theological Seminary traveled with students to Ferguson, Missouri in order to better understand how theology has shaped the movement of #BlackLivesMatter and other urban issues. Our final article in this section is a compilation by Chanequa Walker-Barnes, Oluwatomisin Oredein, AnaYelsi Sanchez, Ginny Giles, and Sandra Van Opstal, who write about their personal experiences as women of color in "What Are All Those Women of Color Doing in That Room? Reflections from the Rainbow."

Finally, we offer three book reviews on works that offer relevant ministry application for the CCDA community. Soong-Chan Rah of North Park Theological Seminary has authored a commentary on the book of Lamentations titled, *Prophetic Lament: A Call for Justice in Troubled Times* (IVP Books, 2015). Old Testament scholar, M. Daniel Carroll R. of Denver Seminary offers a review. Zakiya Jackson offers a review of CCDA CEO, Noel Castellanos' book, *Where the Cross Meets the Streets* and CCDA Journal editor Brandon Wrencher reviews *Dear White Christians*.

EDITORS:
Chanequa Walker-Barnes
Soong-Chan Rah
Brandon Wrencher
Mae Elise Cannon

ON BEHALF OF THE THEOLOGY COMMITTEE OF THE CCDA:
Vince Bantu
M. Daniel Carroll R.
Dominique DuBois Gilliard
Bethany Harris

Part I

CCDA National Conference Theme: "Illuminate"

THE DEFORMED IMAGINATION OF HOW WE ARE LIGHT AND WHAT WE CALL DARKNESS

MIKAEL BROADWAY

When Jesus spoke the words, "I am the light of the world,"[1] no races divided humanity into castes and levels based on pigmentation. People of his era had not imagined race. When Jesus proclaimed, "You are the light of the world,"[2] His listeners did not imagine themselves to be a higher and purer form of the human species because of the color of their skin. When the Fourth Gospel's preamble described a cosmic history of the incarnation, saying, "The light shines in the darkness, and the darkness did not overcome it,"[3] first-century readers inferred no ideology of the white man's burden.

Yet, today, we live in a time when the Biblical language of light and darkness have become encoded upon a system wherein human beings' nature and value are graded according to skin color. Light and darkness language is intertwined with whiteness and blackness. Without attempting to be comprehensive, this essay highlights a few examples and iterations of this misdirection in theology in order to demonstrate its deforming power upon Christian imagination of the church and its mission in the world.

A focal text is Mt 5:14-16, in which Jesus is preaching about the way of life of the disciples. In that context, He speaks of "light" as a hermeneutical key to understanding who the disciples are and how they relate to the marvelous creation in which they live. "You are the light of the world" cannot stand apart from Jesus' very similar statements of "I am the light of the world," found in Jn 8:12 and 9:4-5 (with echoes in 1:3-5 and 12:46). The Messianic and incarnational description of Jesus as the light takes first place theologically, naming Jesus as the source from which light comes to humanity and the world. The Messiah brings the light of God into every place and dimension of creation. It is the very nature of the Incarnate One: "God from God,

1. Jn 8:12; Jn 9:5.

2. Mt 5:14.

3. Jn 1:5.

Light from Light, true God from true God," to shed the light of God abroad "for us and for our salvation."[4]

Matthew's "Sermon on the Mount" describes the hearers and readers of Jesus' words as light. This passage can only be holistically understood as a hermeneutical derivative of Jesus' saying He is Light. As Howard Thurman emphasized, this Jesus who is Light was, a Jew, a poor Jew, and a member of an oppressed minority.[5] The Messianic figure who is Light does not have an accidental social location, but rather was meant to be exactly *this* poor and oppressed Jewish Messiah. This particularity of the "Light of the World" is crucial to how those hearing and reading Jesus' words can accept their own appellation as light. One must root their understanding of Jesus' description of Himself as Light, and secondarily His instructions to His followers to be light, in the Jewish context of Scriptural imagination.

A Brief Review of the Growth of Racialized Theology

A critical divergence, a great appropriation of image and concept, occurred between the writing of the Gospels and the modern globalization of European theo-politics. Although there is no single moment of beginning, a watershed coalescence of circumstances, events, structures, and ideas have recreated the Christian imagination of the world. Christian understanding of "light" and "darkness" became intertwined with the ambitions of European nations and cultures for world domination. Ambition and ethnocentricity dissolved the particularity of the Jewish Jesus who was proclaiming the light of the God of Israel and shining forth in those who have received that light and become its beacons. A new age restructured the church's mission into transplanting European power, peoples, and culture into the rest of the world. Superseding the lowly Jewish Messiah and occluding the particular Light of that Word made flesh, light became the sovereignty of European empire and culture to be transplanted and colonized in all places, even through force of arms and mass extermination of peoples.[6]

European kingdoms emerged from the Middle Ages with a strong sense of themselves as the bearers of Christian identity, having carried on centuries of conflict against Islamic encroachment on the ancient homelands of the Christian church. New possibilities in oceanic navigation were leading to encounters with peoples on other continents. On the level of interpersonal contact, the outcome of these encounters held many possibilities. Mutual exchange, openness, hospitality, friendship—these

4. "The Nicene Creed," *The Episcopal Church: The Creeds* (accessed at http://www.episcopalchurch.org/page/creeds on July 25, 2015).

5. Howard Thurman, *Jesus and the Disinherited* (Boston: Beacon Press, 1949), 15-18.

6. I owe a debt to many colleagues for the concepts which frame this essay, in particular to J. Kameron Carter, Willie J. Jennings, J. Deotis Roberts, and Luis N. Rivera, whose works are cited below, as well as to James H. Cone, *The Cross and the Lynching Tree* (Maryknoll, NY: Orbis Books, 2011), and M. Shawn Copeland, *Enfleshing Freedom* (Minneapolis: Fortress Press, 2009).

were all contingent possibilities. Of course, conflict, rivalry, domination, and exploitation were also possible.

Entering upon the early stages of modernity, these European kingdoms had ambitions for empire and the power and wealth it could mean. Because European church leadership was hoping to regain its power of primacy and to participate in the imperial expansion, Pope Alexander issued bulls granting expansive powers over all overseas lands to the Catholic monarchs of Europe.[7] A Eurocentric worldview, greed for land and riches, and rivalry among emerging states seeking imperial power combined to link Christian identity to imperial expansion. These power relations affected the possibilities for encounter such that European travelers became biased toward seeing people and lands primarily for their commercial value. Christopher Columbus's widely known response to meeting people in the Caribbean was to make note in his journal about their usefulness for slave labor.

Columbus and others of his era, whether Catholic or Protestant, understood their work to be fully intertwined with the spread of Christian faith, and their conceptual and practical linking of faith and conquest appears everywhere in their written accounts. These encounters between light-skinned Europeans and others with different skin tones from Africa and the Americas began to take on a complexity of meanings. Accustomed to the appearance of their neighbors in their homelands, travelers from Europe judged the appearance of others by its departure from that norm, that standard of beauty. As J. Deotis Roberts wrote, "Color takes on aesthetic and ethical meaning. Black is considered ugly and bad; white is considered beautiful and good."[8] The logical structures around these foci continuously gather to themselves polarized terms of value, with white always the favorable and superior and black always the unfavorable and inferior. This logic continues to inhabit the imagination of contemporary Christianity.

Massachusetts Bay Colony, Puritan Theology, and Being a "Citty [sic] Upon a Hill"

A pivotal historic citation of Mt 5:14-16 appears in John Winthrop's sermon delivered shipboard in 1630, while at sea en route to New England. He tells the colonists on the Arbella, "We shall be as a citty [sic] upon a hill," then adds "The eies [sic] of all people are uppon [sic] us."[9] He portrays their future settlement as a beacon of light for the ways of God. People are watching *especially them* to see whether there is a true witness of God's purpose for the world.

7. Luis N. Rivera, *A Violent Evangelism* (Louisville: WJKP, 1992), 26-29.

8. J. Deotis Roberts, *A Black Political Theology* (Louisville: WJKP, 2005) 28.

9. John Winthrop, "A Modell of Christian Charity," Collections of the Massachusetts Historical Society, 3rd series (Boston, 1838) 7:31-48 (accessed at Hanover Historical Texts Project, http://history.hanover.edu/texts/winthmod.html, July 1, 2015).

In the background of his sermon lie other critical documents besides the Bible: the Charter of the Massachusetts Bay Company and the Constitution of Massachusetts Bay Colony. These documents frame their mission within the commercial and imperial purposes of the wealthy merchants and rulers of England.[10] Regulating eyes are upon them, watching with a normative gaze of European expansion. Of course, those who had strong religious fervor also expected all reform-minded Christians to be watching from Europe. But the critical watching eyes are those with commercial and imperial ambition. Can this colony produce wealth? Can they expand the sovereign power and territory of the King? Under the Charter, Winthrop is calling for planting this settlement and "succeeding plantations" so that people will praise God that a "*New England*" has begun to emerge, by implication both larger and better. A supersessionist theology baptizes the commercial and colonial interests of empire, including authorizing civil rule and militarization.

Mostly absent from this interpretation of Matthew 5 are the eyes of the previous inhabitants of North America. Far down the order of priority of the colonists' mission is shining a light toward new neighbors. Prior residents will be watching the settling, appropriation, militarization, and claims of sovereignty that materialize. One might protest that one sermon cannot contain all Winthrop's convictions about missiology, yet this text and its background documents would point to the conclusion that any light the prior residents see will offer only subjugation, a package deal made up of the dogma, the business, the hierarchies, and the domination systems of these who claim to be the new rulers of this land.

In this absence we become aware of the deep structural causes of modern racialized existence, as described by J. Kameron Carter. Following the pattern of Jewish counter history exhibited in the Old Testament, the Puritans see themselves as being liberated from the sovereignty of corrupted empires, both Catholic and English. Yet at the same time they manifest the transition within modernity toward a new kind of sovereignty of nation, of people, replacing the sovereignty embodied in the ruler. This new emergent sovereignty leaves much unsaid in its machinations of production and reproduction. In addition to defending against the external threats of other Christian princes or nations, a new form of biopower was becoming a decentralized mode of inward purification, based on classifying humanity according to bodily differences.[11] Were immigrants and prior residents to occupy the same space, it would be critical to maintain purity of the nation. Transplanting the Jewish problem into a land with no Jews, these and other early modern colonists share in creating the modern idea and structure of race. As Europe had to be purged of the impurity of Jews, so now the logic

10. "The Charter of the Massachusetts Bay Company," *The Winthrop Society: Texts* (accessed at http://winthropsociety.com/doc_charter.php, July 10, 2015); see also "The Constitution of the Massachusetts Bay Plantation," *Winthrop Society* (accessed at http://winthropsociety.com/doc_const.php, July 10, 2015).

11. J. Kameron Carter, *Race: A Theological Account* (New York: Oxford University Press, 2008), 54–55, 65–67.

and nature of the modern nation would lead to the necessity of purging colonized lands of their impure peoples.

The wider context of missiological framing of English colonialism of North America reveals a sweeping supersessionism. Colonizers described their situation as parallel to that of Abraham and Sarah, having been given a land within which to dwell. They saw themselves often in the role of Joshua, driving out the evil Canaanites and possessing the land.[12] This missiology of displacement and replacement, of extermination and purification, found cultural prominence, even when later generations stripped it of overt Christian doctrinal or Scriptural language. From Israel and the British Mandate of Palestine, to Manifest Destiny, to American Exceptionalism and "the last best hope of the world,"[13] the modern nation retains theological power as a doctrine of salvation. The people, the nation, even all humanity can be saved through defeat or subjection of all enemies external and internal. Devotion to the national project and identity transformed the meaning of light theologically, so that it comes to be aligned with a racialized world and a providential battle for civilization.

Light and Darkness Deformed

George Freeman, a Massachusetts native who served as rector of Christ Church, Raleigh, NC, delivered widely read treatises on slavery in 1836. Although condemning the evils of the slave trade, he opposed emancipation on missiological grounds. Citing the so-called "curse of Ham" prophecy, he concludes that slavery in

> *the present day, is agreeable to the order of Divine Providence.* But further; taken in connexion [sic] with these views of the prophetic sentence of Noah, and these statements of the actual condition of the debased natives of Africa for many ages, does it not appear that it was, upon the whole, (to *them*, however it may be considered in regard to *us*) a *merciful Providence*, which led to the removal of such large numbers of that wretched people from their own inhospitable and barbarous country, and their transplantation into *this land of peace, of security, of abundance, of civilization, and of Christian light?* [emphasis mine][14]

He claimed that by participating, even tangentially, in the civilization planted on North American soil by English and other European colonizers, Africans were better off.

12. See Bruce E. Trigger and Wilcomb E. Washburn, *The Cambridge History of the Native Peoples of the Americas*, Part 1 (Cambridge: Cambridge University Press, 1996), 76-77.

13. Larry E. Tise, whose research has been very helpful in identifying historical sources, argues that the justifications and social construction of slavocracy have their origins in New England, citing messianic visions of peoplehood in authors such as Timothy Dwight, in *Proslavery: A History of the Defense of Slavery in America, 1701-1840* (Athens, GA: University of Georgia Press, 2011), 208.

14. George Freeman, *The Rights and Duties of Slave-holders*" (Charleston: A.E. Miller, printer to the society, 1837), 17-18.

"Debased" in their homeland, they were being saved by being kidnapped, shipped as cargo, sold, and enslaved perpetually. Looking upon their captors, overseers, and owners, they could behold the light. These treatises demonstrate how light continued to be deformed for missiology in the modern world and particularly in North America.

Freeman's argument also illustrates the "white man's burden"[15] by portraying the mission of the church as identical with the mission of advancing Western civilization and power. Lesser peoples, ranked according to physical appearance with darker-skinned people at the lowest level, must be elevated by the higher peoples, with European whites at the apex of humanity. As Sandy Martin points out, missionaries like Thomas Jefferson Bowen, writing in the 1850s, accepted the view "that God had chosen the white race as tutor for the African race." Thus, Bowen could argue for displacement of native cultures through the enlightening power of Western civilization.

> There must be a somewhat extensive diffusion of correct science, a knowledge of the world and its history, just notions of civil government, some proficiency in the arts which are indispensible to enlightened men, commerce, and above all, the sanctifying influence of Christianity, all cooperating before we can reasonably hope for the conversion and elevation of any people.[16]

The giddiness of Western societies for cultural and political expansion in the late nineteenth century led to many missiological writings about the future of Africa, often called the Dark Continent. *Dawn in the Dark Continent* stated, "Long the least known and least developed, the most neglected and most despised of all continents, Africa has suddenly emerged into the light of day. The time is not far distant when it will be a great field of human enterprise and activity." Here, James Stewart uses imagery of light as a sign of the spread of Christian faith, while discussing the vigorous efforts of European nations to claim lands for empire and colonization in Africa.[17]

Stewart's words demand careful examination. To whom was the African continent least known? On whose scale was it least developed? By whom was it most neglected, and by whom despised? As with Winthrop, the missiological vision continues to be dominated by the normative gaze of whiteness. Lacking whites and white culture, the continent is dark. It is dark because of the darkness of people's skin, a sign of their inferiority. It is dark because it is unknown, and assumed to be available for appropriation—an open canvas, a virgin land. Willie Jennings points out that this Enlightenment imagination of the world displaces peoples and landscapes for

15. A poem encouraging the U.S. colonization of The Philippines after the Spanish-American War popularized this term; see Rudyard Kipling, "The White Man's Burden: The United States and the Philippine Islands, 1899," *Internet Modern History Sourcebook* (accessed at http://www.fordham.edu/halsall/mod/kipling.asp, July 30, 2015).

16. Sandy D. Martin, *Black Baptists and African Missions* (Macon, GA: Mercer University Press, 1989), 29-30.

17. James Stewart, *Dawn in the Dark Continent; or Africa and Its Missions* (New York: Fleming H. Revell, 1903), 357.

the sake of remaking remote colonies in the likeness of the colonizers' homelands. It offers a racialized soteriology enacted through "dislodging particular identities from particular places," reshaping African existence with Western "humane, Christianized domesticity." Jennings calls this the "whiteness hermeneutic," the vision of bringing light to the world by reshaping the world in the image of white societies.[18]

Patrick Brantlinger argues that after the era of abolitionism, which led to the end of the British slave trade, Victorian sensibilities reshaped British identity as "the potential saviors of the African." Accustomed to reading of the horrors of the slave trade in Africa, a more general view of Africa's degradation took hold. A new kind of literature made heroes of the wealthy British explorers and exploiters of Africa who moved:

> from adventure to adventure against a dark, infernal backdrop where there are no other characters of equal stature—only bewitched or demonic savages.. . . [E]xplorers usually portray them as amusing or dangerous obstacles or as objects of curiosity, while missionaries usually portray Africans as weak, pitiable, inferior mortals who need to be shown the light.[19]

As imagined Africa became more intensely dark, Europeans' mission to bring light grew more urgent. Ranking races by their nearness to this light or whiteness, it was not uncommon for Europeans to doubt the possibility of redeeming or improving the Africans. Many concluded that evolutionary social progress, carried out through displacement, eugenics, or genocide, would be the proper path.[20]

> Africa grew "dark" as Victorian explorers, missionaries, and scientists flooded it with light, because the light was refracted through an imperialist ideology that urged the abolition of "savage customs" in the name of civilization. As a product of that ideology, the myth of the Dark Continent developed.[21]

Some might object that the criticisms in this essay address an old problem and one that has been adequately resolved in past decades. Yet such ideas and structures do not easily disappear. The work of Michelle Alexander and others has provided extensive evidence of the racial disparity in policing, prosecution, and prisons.[22] The Black Lives Matter movement has grown out of widespread impunity for those who kill unarmed black people.[23] The massacre of black worshipers in Charleston, South

18. Willie J. Jennings, *The Christian Imagination* (New Haven, CT: Yale University Press, 2010), 136-39.

19. Patrick Brantlinger, "Victorians and Africans: The Genealogy of the Myth of the Dark Continent," 166-203 in *Race, Writing, and Difference*, ed. by Henry Louis Gates and Anthony Appiah (Chicago: University of Chicago Press, 1985), 176-78.

20. Ibid. 186.

21. Ibid. 166.

22. Michelle Alexander, *The New Jim Crow* (New York: New Press, 2010); see also Alan Bean's work at "Friends of Justice" (accessed at https://friendsofjustice.wordpress.com on July 31, 2015).

23. "Black Lives Matter" (accessed at http://blacklivesmatter.com on July 31, 2015).

Carolina, brought evidence of the prevalence of white supremacist ideology and organizing in the U.S.[24] Life and death remain in the balance, with dark bodies marked for death. To this day, some Christian mission organizations continue to use light and darkness language in ways rooted in white supremacy, such as this one: "There are many other opportunities for ministry on the Dark Continent, as the door is open in most countries to minister openly and freely."[25]

Light on Gospel Terms

Other sources in contemporary missiology have converted their use of light to bring greater conformity to the Gospel. For instance, the Micah Network offers an agenda for missiological practice of leaders and churches. Linking texts from Jeremiah and Matthew, one mandate for church mission says, "to seek the welfare of cities, acting together to be salt and light."[26] Light, referencing Mt 5:13-16, is the final word in a series of statements for ecclesial calling that includes peacemaking, seeking justice, promoting equality and dignity of all, and generous economic sharing. Elsewhere, Pak Tan further elaborates this missiological use of light. After quoting Mt 15:16, he brings the focus to "Doing good works in the name of God," elaborating on its specifying various forms of community development ministry in nutrition, housing, health, education, recovery, and relief.[27] Thus, the Micah Network offers examples of missiological reflection, which brings the term light more clearly in line with the hermeneutical key of Jesus' own words.

Tan brings to the foreground something Winthrop also saw in the Mt 5 text: light should reveal good works. While Winthrop focused his discussion on the good works shown toward fellow plantation settlers, Tan has in mind more permeable boundaries of community. The good works he describes serve the church and all its neighbors, all sharing in the commonweal.

Jesus' words about light in Mt 5 follow the opening of the Sermon on the Mount, in which He has described the character of a Christian way of life. The Beatitudes enumerate a core of the good works to which Jesus refers. While it is popular to use cute terms such as "be-attitudes" as part of the positive thinking ideology of contemporary Christian rhetoric, the actual list of virtues is far from inwardly focused. Meekness,

24. Michael McLaughlin, "Racist Manifesto Purportedly Written by Dylann Roof Surfaces Online," *Huffington Post* (accessed at http://www.huffingtonpost.com/2015/06/20/dylann-roof-manifesto-charleston-shooting_n_7627788.html on August 4, 2015).

25. "Africa," *ABWE International* website (accessed at http://www.abwe.org/serve/regions/africa, July 1, 2015).

26. "Micah Call to Action 2014," *Micah Network* website (accessed at http://www.micahnetwork.org/news/micah-call-action-2014, June 5, 2015).

27. Pak Tan, "Grace, Faith, and Good Works—A Biblical Reflection," *Micah Network* website, quoted from *Care Contact*, March-May 2014 (accessed at http://www.micahnetwork.org/news/grace-faith-and-good-works, June 5, 2015).

mourning, purity of heart, poverty of spirit—these terms might be construed as more inward; however, they are linked with peacemaking, hunger and thirst for justice, mercy, and standing up for right even to the point of suffering. Only a distortion of the text allows Jesus' sayings about a blessed life to be reduced to inward feelings or thoughts. They are relational and even structural in their orientation. The good works that shine as a light are works done for the sake of the neighbor. There is no evidence of hungering for justice without doing justice and seeking justice. Pushback and persecution respond to active virtues, not passivity. Jesus is describing a life that takes up a cross to follow. This poor, oppressed Jew did not call for works of justice defined by imperial interest or colonial displacement. The good works that are good news seek the common good, not merely the good of the dominant group, the colonial power, or the fair-skinned neighbor.

The theology Jesus learned and embodied was rooted in the Jewish tradition. When he spoke of light, the concept would reside within a Scriptural imagination. Attentive Bible readers will know that Jesus often quoted the Hebrew Scriptures, especially drawing on the Torah books of Exodus and Deuteronomy, the Psalms, and the Prophet Isaiah. From these scrolls, Jesus would have learned a symbology of light which tells the story of God's shaping Israel to be a people in God's own image. Many times throughout the Old Testament the word light points to daily living, conveying the importance of light for life and human flourishing. It is no surprise that Jewish theologians told the story of creation as rooted in a Word directly from the essence of God, which began its evangel with, "Let there be light."

The stories from the Torah emphasize light as the presence of God. By night, God's presence to the children of Israel was through a pillar of fire, a light for them to look upon. Many instructions concerning building the Tabernacle focused on keeping a lamp lit as a sign of God's presence. The Psalms note the light of God as a sign of presence that is embedded in the very creation. The world in which God has placed humanity is full of goodness. The ways of God in the earth are marked by justice. God's love springs forth in all creation. Ps. 112 associates light with the godly life of generosity and justice, of caring for the poor and trusting God in all things. Ps. 119 prays for the light of God to guide into just, right living.

The Prophet Isaiah links light to the inbreaking power of God to set things right. The light comes to break oppression and to stop violence. Chapters 9 and 42 link light to the Messianic hope, looking to the day when God's servant will not rest until justice has been established. Is 42:6-7, "I will give you as a covenant for the people, a light for the nations, to open the eyes that are blind, to bring out the prisoners from the dungeon, from the prison those who sit in darkness," echoes the words Jesus read from chapter 61 of the Isaiah scroll as he announced his program for ministry. The prophet's oracle in chapter 51 says, "I will set my justice for a light to the peoples." Light and justice repeatedly appear as parallel concepts. To be in the presence of God's light is to be in the presence of God's justice. Thus, Isaiah's pivotal oracle of justice in chapter 58 twice (vv 8 and 10) links the blessing and flourishing of God's people with establishing economic and political justice by making sure people have homes, caring for families and neighbors, sharing food, sharing clothing, and breaking the yoke of oppression. Chapters 60-61 describe the shining light of God's people upon whom all nations will look as a great era of flourishing characterized by good news for the poor and oppressed.

If light is a sign of God's presence with and in creation, then whatever light God's people might claim to have must be fully in concord with the nature of God's own light. The biblical link between justice as the revealed nature of God and the created nature of humanity must never be severed. To read the words, "You are the light of the world," with integrity and faithfulness, the light of the church must display itself in working for justice for all creation. Any attempt to enclose the light in tribal, ethnic, racial, and similar limitations is a denial of the Christian gospel.

Bibliography

ABWE International. "Africa." http://www.abwe.org/serve/regions/africa (accessed July 1, 2015).

Black Lives Matter. http://blacklivesmatter.com (accessed July 31, 2015).

Brantlinger, Patrick. "Victorians and Africans: The Genealogy of the Myth of the Dark Continent." In *Race, Writing, and Difference*, ed. by Henry Louis Gates and Anthony Appiah, 176-178. Chicago: University of Chicago Press, 1985.

Carter, J. Kameron. *Race: A Theological Account*. New York: Oxford University Press, 2008.

Dwight, Timothy. *Proslavery: A History of the Defense of Slavery in America, 1701-1840*. Athens, GA: University of Georgia Press, 2011.

Freeman, George *The Rights and Duties of Slave-holders*" Charleston: A.E. Miller, printer to the society, 1837.

Jennings, Willie J. *The Christian Imagination*. New Haven, CT: Yale University Press, 2010.

Kipling, Rudyard. "The White Man's Burden: The United States and the Philippine Islands, 1899," Internet Modern History Sourcebook. http://www.fordham.edu/halsall/mod/kipling.asp (accessed July 30, 2015).

Martin, Sandy D. *Black Baptists and African Missions*. Macon, GA: Mercer University Press, 1989.

McLaughlin, Michael. "Racist Manifesto Purportedly Written by Dylann Roof Surfaces Online." *Huffington Post*. http://www.huffingtonpost.com/2015/06/20/dylann-roof-manifesto-charleston-shooting_n_7627788.html (accessed August 4, 2015).

Micah Network. "Care Contact." http://www.micahnetwork.org/news/grace-faith-and-good- works (accessed June 5, 2015).

Micah Network. "Micah Call to Action 2014." http://www.micahnetwork.org/news/micah-call-action-2014 (accessed at, June 5, 2015).

Michelle Alexander, *The New Jim Crow* (New York: New Press, 2010); see also Alan Bean's work at "Friends of Justice" (accessed at https://friendsofjustice.wordpress.com on July 31, 2015).

Rivera, Luis N. *A Violent Evangelism*. Louisville: WJKP, 1992.

Roberts, J. Deotis. *A Black Political Theology*. Louisville: WJKP, 2005.

Stewart, James. *Dawn in the Dark Continent; or Africa and Its Missions*. New York: Fleming H. Revell, 1903.

The Episcopal Church: The Creeds, "The Nicene Creed." http://www.episcopalchurch.org/page/creeds (accessed July 25, 2015).

The Winthrop Society: Texts, "The Charter of the Massachusetts Bay Company."

http://winthropsociety.com/doc_charter.php (accessed at, July 10, 2015)

Thurman, Howard. *Jesus and the Disinherited.* Boston: Beacon Press, 1949.

Trigger, Bruce E. and Washburn, Wilcomb E. *The Cambridge History of the Native Peoples of the Americas,* Part 1. Cambridge: Cambridge University Press, 1996.

Winthrop Society, "The Constitution of the Massachusetts Bay Plantation." http://winthropsociety.com/doc_const.php (accessed July 10, 2015).

Winthrop, John, "A Modell of Christian Charity," Collections of the Massachusetts Historical Society, 3rd series. http://history.hanover.edu/texts/winthmod.html (accessed July 1, 2015).

THE LIGHT SHINES IN THE DARKNESS
SOME IMPLICATIONS OF JOHN'S THEOLOGY OF LIGHT FOR CCD

JOSHUA BECKETT

Throughout this year's national conference we will be considering together what it means to "embody the light of Christ, illuminating the darkness, exposing injustice and shining light on the movement of God's kingdom, bringing one another into the radiant light of transformation."[1] Such reflections, nurtured by instruction from the Sermon on the Mount, are critically important for rightly understanding our identity and faithfully stepping into our mission in the midst of confusing times. Specifically, our theme passage of Matthew 5:14–16 emphasizes the significance of human agency. That is, the way that we shine matters, not only for our own lives and those close to us, but even for people currently outside of our communities. In a society where systemic injustice has caused many people to wonder whether their lives—let alone their actions and voices—matter, this is a liberating and empowering message that deserves widespread attention.

Yet there are also dangers associated with hearing the clarion call: "You are the light of the world!" To begin with, we often overlook the fact that Jesus is addressing a community, and we instead individualize the corporate "you" (whereas *hymeis* in Matt 5:14 is plural). Such a move, unconscious as it is, can fuel both isolation and idolatry. As community leaders, activists, volunteers, pastors, and teachers, we know that it can be easy to lose sight of the sober dignity and joyful responsibility of Jesus' declaration and instead slip into prideful self-importance (in the name of "kingdom ministry," of course). Forgetting where the light comes from, or acting like we own the light, does not usually end well. As perhaps some of this year's conference attendees can testify, although a city on a hill cannot be hidden, it can experience burnout!

1. CCDA website. http://www.ccda.org/events/national-conferences. Accessed June 24, 2015.8

Thankfully, among the Gospels, different evangelists conceive of and employ the theme of light in surprisingly distinct ways. While Matthew highlights human responsibility in maintaining and propagating our light, John reminds us that our actions find their meaning and gain their coherence "in light of" the reality of Jesus, the original and ultimate light of the world, in whose identity and mission we participate. When taken together, Matthew and John offer us an intriguing, fruitful tension that illuminates our attempts to shine forth God's light in the world.

In this short essay, I will particularly expound on three Johannine passages: the Prologue (chapter 1), the editorial comments after Jesus' nocturnal discussion with Nicodemus (chapter 3), and Jesus' response to the report of Gentiles seeking to meet him during Passover (chapter 12). In each case, John contrasts Jesus' identity as the light that comes into the world with the "darkness." In each case, there is a corresponding call to a discipleship of belief and action ("receive", "come", and "walk", respectively). And in each case, there are implications for the contemporary practice of Christian Community Development (CCD) that I would like to explore. Specifically, I will address the questions of the nature and scope of our mission (John 1), the challenge of responding to opposition with conviction but without judgment (John 3), and the call to cross-cultural barriers (John 12).

The Theme of Light in Matthew

First, however, a further word on Matthew's use of light is in order. The two major clusters of light-related language[2] in this Gospel both appear in the Sermon on the Mount. The first is our aforementioned theme passage, in which Matthew sets symbolic examples of human-created brilliance (a city on a hill and a lamp on a stand) in parallel with the righteous deeds of his listening, obedient disciples. "In the same way"[3] that these entities illuminate their surroundings for the benefit of others, the actions of Jesus-followers should catch the attention of other people, all to the glory of God. Later in the Sermon, Matthew reports Jesus' sobering words about the eye as the lamp of the body (6:22–23). As goes the eye, so follows the rest of the body, for light or for darkness. Although symbolic in language, the ethical force of this passage is clear (which relates to the immediately preceding teaching about the heart's treasure).

The handful of other occurrences of light and its synonyms in Matthew are more literal in their reference to visible brilliance. These include: Jesus' missional charge for his disciples to tell in the light what they heard from him in the dark (10:27), his apocalyptic description of the cosmic announcement of his coming (24:27–29), and

2. Most of these instances involve *phōs*, a common word for light. However, a few other similar words make an appearance: *phōteinos* (related to *phōs*) in Matt 6:22, *astraphē* ("lightning", 24:27) and *phengos* ("radiance", 24:29) in Matthew's apocalypse.

3. Of course, there is also a parallel with salt: the gathered disciples are the salt of the earth, preserving and flavoring their environment. But there is another contrast here as well: once salt loses its saltiness, it cannot be made salty again, whereas light cannot be hidden in the first place.

his transfiguration (17:2) and resurrection (28:3) appearances. Thus on the whole, when Matthew writes of light literally, he relates it directly to the person or message of Jesus, whereas his more figurative uses tend to be related to the nature and activity of Jesus' followers.[4]

The Theme of Light in John

By contrast, the Fourth Gospel offers a consistently symbolic presentation of light and almost exclusively relates it to the person of Jesus.[5] Light both frames and fills John's Book of Signs[6] and becomes a central motif in Johannine Christology. Throughout the first twelve chapters, John connects light with several of his other favorite themes: creation, the world, glory, life, judgment, witness, grace and truth, reception and belief, Jesus' coming and going, and the universal and particular. Significantly, John twice reports Jesus appropriating light to his own identity with the powerful declaration "I am the light of the world."[7] Among the multiple expressions of the language and concept of light in the Fourth Gospel, there are three major clusters: one each at the beginning and end of the Book of Signs, and another following the Bible's most famous verse.[8] To these passages, and their weighty bearing on Christian Community Development, we now turn.

Prologue (1:1–18)

The Fourth Gospel begins with a sweeping account of the Word's preexistence, proximity to and identity with God, and exclusive role as the agent of creation (1:1–3). Then the narrative shifts to focus on the Word's intrinsic life that was light for all people, unconquered by the darkness (1:4–5). God also sent John as a witness so that all might believe in the true light, which gives light to every person and was coming in the world (1:6–9). Although the world didn't recognize him as its maker, and although his own people didn't receive him as their master, the Word became flesh: moving into

4. One exception to this pattern occurs in Matthew 4:16, which quotes Isaiah 9:2 ("the people living in darkness have seen a great light"). The figurative use of light is related to the teaching ministry of Jesus in mixed Jewish/Gentile territory, and it fits well with Matthew's theme of Jesus fulfilling the Scriptures.

5. The exception that proves the rule occurs in John 5:35, in which Jesus refers to John the Baptist as a burning and shining lamp (*ho luchnos ho kaiomenos kai phainōn*). However, given the closeness between the message of John and the light of Jesus, even this passage has profound Christological significance.

6. Many have divided the Fourth Gospel into the Book of Signs (1–12) and the Book of Glory (13–21).

7. 8:12 and 9:5. Throughout John, "I am" statements offer strong indications about Jesus' identity, often connected with his miracles.

8. At least if evangelistic crusades and sporting events are any indication!

humanity's neighborhood, revealing the Son's glory of grace and truth, and granting adoption into God's family to all who believed in him (1:10–14).

The scope of the mission of Jesus is breathtakingly expansive! In this supreme act of relocation, the unique Son of God's mission to one particular people, the fullness of God's universal love for all people becomes manifest. This has profound implications for CCD. To begin with, it promotes a humble confidence in divine agency: all the darkness in the world cannot snuff out the radiance of God's light, which is already at work illuminating all people.[9] It also reminds us that at the heart of the cosmic relocation of the Incarnation was a passion for expanding God's family. Thus, a crucial element of the "wholistic" ministry that we seek to promote is God's call to adoption through believing in the name of Christ. Finally, it removes from us the pressure of creating the light (God's prerogative); rather, our role (like John's) is to bear witness to others about the light that we have seen.

Commentary after Nicodemus (3:16–21)

The second major section on light in the Gospel of John comes after Jesus' wide-ranging conversation (about seeing and entering the kingdom, being born of water and Spirit, and knowing and accepting his testimony) with the Pharisee Nicodemus. Although some people have taken these verses as a continuation of the words of Jesus, they are probably better rendered as John's own theological commentary on the matter. After the familiar words of John 3:16—which remain astounding in their proclamation of God's universal love—comes a series of stark contrasts in rapid succession: salvation, not condemnation, as the Father's purpose in sending the Son (3:17); no condemnation for believers, but (self-)condemnation for nonbelievers on the grounds of their unbelief (3:18); light has come, but love of the darkness leads people to reject it (3:19); and evildoers avoid the light so that their deeds will not be exposed, while truthdoers seek the light so that their deeds will be vindicated (3:20–21).

What does this mean for our work of restoring under-resourced communities? A few consequences follow from this potent passage. To begin with, we need to face the reality that one of the largest obstacles toward Christian ministry of any kind is our reputation for being swifter to deal out condemnation than to emulate the compassion of Jesus. There are multiple reasons for why this reputation has developed, and not all of them are fair. Nevertheless, in order to rectify this tragic state of affairs, it is essential that we squarely acknowledge it and repent from our own complicity in such condemnation. Secondly, we need to prepare for opposition.[10] Even though

9. Some theologians, such as the drafters of the Vatican II document *Lumen Gentium*, consider John 1:9 (among other passages) to entail soteriological inclusivism (that is, all people are saved through Christ). For my part, such a move exceeds its exegetical basis; however, I think we can at least say that the light of Christ reaches out to people before and beyond any human witnesses to him (as significant as these are in God's purposes).

10. From the outset it should be acknowledged that opposition may take many forms: the vested

Jesus' own pattern in the world was not one of condemnation, his light provoked a crisis of decision in others: turning to him in belief and action or rejecting him for the injury his light wrought to their deeds and motives. Many chose the latter course of opposition, even to the point of conspiring to destroy him. We who follow Jesus in his ministry of reconciliation should not expect a different result, but rather are called to take up his example of loving the haters. Finally, although condemnation is not our prerogative, holiness is our mandate. If we wish to testify to the brilliantly illuminating, decision-provoking light of Christ with integrity, we must cultivate a distinctive love of truth and goodness in our own lives, communities, and ministries.

Gentiles at the Feast (12:20–36)

The final words on light in the Gospel of John appear right at the beginning of the series of events leading to Jesus' crucifixion during the Passover festival. After the raising of Lazarus, Mary of Bethany's anointing, and the Humble Entry into Jerusalem,[11] John narrates an account of Greeks asking Philip (a Jewish disciple with a Greek name) if they could see Jesus. When Philip and Andrew relay this request to Jesus, his response initially appears to ignore it altogether, speaking instead about the time for his glorification, the fruit-bearing death of a kernel of wheat, his closeness with his servants, and his desire that his Father be glorified (accompanied by a voice from heaven that the crowd confuses with thunder or an angel). In fact, we have no textual evidence that the Greeks in question ever gained their opportunity for the audience that they had sought. But Jesus does indeed address their desire, prophesying that his atoning death will be the means of God's grace to be distributed far and wide: "And I, when I am lifted up from the earth, will draw all people to myself" (12:32). Then he warns all of his listeners that the light (in this case, his physical presence) will not be with them much longer, and he calls them to walk in the light and put their trust in the light while it is with them,[12] so that they may become children of light.

Reading and reflecting on these words from our vantage point, between the resurrection and return of Jesus, we find an implicit cruciform imperative to cross-cultural ministry. As with the other Johannine passages, the decisive work has been done by Jesus, but since "whoever serves me must follow me; and where I am, my

interests of powerful people and corporations who benefit from unjust structures, general animosity due to our impoverished, culture war mentality-ridden public discourse, and the painful phenomenon of "friendly fire" within Christian churches, ministries, and networks. Recipients of these and other forms of opposition could all stand to hear John's reminder.

11. I prefer this designation to the Triumphal Entry, which may be an indication of our profound temptation to make God in our own image. Like the disciples, we want a warrior king astride a great horse; but what Jesus offers instead is a humble servant king on a donkey, whose greatness is shown in his humility and self-sacrifice.

12. This is quite similar to John 11:9–10, in the context of a conversation with his disciples after the death of Lazarus.

servant also will be" (12:26), we participate as well. It is clear that the drawing of all peoples to the knowledge of Jesus is a top priority; living together as the united people of God is just as urgent an ambition. For far too long many Christians have become complacent about the scandal of churches succumbing to and mirroring (rather than challenging and transcending) the segregated patterns of our broken society.

Additionally, the resurrection remains a source of hope and joy throughout our ministry struggles, just as Christ's return sharpens our focus and urgency. We emulate his model of self-giving love and lay down our lives for others, even as we trust that our small, often futile efforts will bear much fruit. Such a mundane, agricultural model is certainly a challenge to our perpetual tendency toward hubris and vainglory in mission! But it is also a source of hope that our ministry, which can often seem nearly dead, never really ends in failure. With sobriety and gratitude, we can hear and respond to the words of Jesus: "I have come into the world as a light, so that no one who believes in me should stay in darkness" (12:46).

Conclusion: Bringing Johannine and Matthean Light Together[13]

As this brief survey and reflection demonstrates, John's theology of light is without exception metaphorical and figurative, and is always directly linked with Jesus. The Johannine accent falls squarely on the sovereign agency and effective power of God. For Matthew, symbolic light language refers to Jesus' followers, while he reserves his literal representations of light for Jesus. Both approaches are present in the New Testament, and both are necessary for our proper formation and ministry, though we are in danger if we only incorporate one lens. Some people—perhaps scholars and writers who are not serving in the trenches of CCD—need to be reminded of the necessity of Matthew's call to be the light of the world. Others—perhaps sleeves-rolled-up activists and pastors who are tempted to delusion about the indispensability or brilliance of their own light—need to hear afresh the truth that Jesus, the unique Son of the Father, is the light of the world and the source of any light we may have. We need one another to live out our identity as the light of the world, always remembering its source.

Ultimately, Matthew's and John's theologies of light come together for us in a powerful synthesis. It is because of the uniqueness of the Incarnation that our ministry can be "incarnational." It is because the light has come and provoked the world's self-incriminating verdict that we can serve with conviction and without judgment. It is because the true light has overcome the darkness by laying down his own life that we can follow him in a costly journey of self-giving love. And in the end, it is because Jesus is the light of the world that we too can shine brightly within it.

13. I would like to thank Justin Bailey and Jennifer Aycock for their constructive and critical comments on an earlier draft of this paper.

BE THE LIGHT
ILLUMINATION TOWARD RACIAL JUSTICE

LIZ MOSBO-VERHAGE

"You are the light of the world. A city built on a hill cannot be hid. No one after lighting a lamp puts it under the bushel basket, but on the lampstand, and it gives light to all in the house. In the same way, let your light shine before others, so that they may see your good works and give glory to your Father in heaven."

MATTHEW 5:14-16

Illumination as Justice: Understanding the Text

This text from Matthew points us to a popular passage right on the heels of the Beatitudes. Earlier in this chapter Jesus has been proclaiming who will be blessed and who God rewards—and it has radical, counter-cultural, and mind-blowing implications. In the Beatitudes, social categories were turned on their heads, expectations were shifted, the weaker and more vulnerable populations were given places of honor and reward. Christ concludes this teaching with these metaphors about God's people being salt and light. Followers of Jesus are told they are a distinct people, assigned radical, counter-cultural tasks, who will now also be a witness and impact the rest of society. Followers of Jesus have flavor and preserve as salt does, and they illuminate the way and beckon others from far off as light does in the dark. We in the church have this unique call to live out the radical teachings of what God blesses—mourning, meekness, mercy, peacemaking, those who hunger and thirst for righteousness/justice, those who are persecuted—and then we are told to share that calling with the world.

These metaphors are some of my favorite depictions of the church in the Bible—and understandably, many of us in the church often use these easy-to-understand pictures of salt and light. Dr. Emerson Powery of Messiah College reminds us, however, that these well-loved metaphors are not simply illustrations - they are instead categories of being, marking the identity and practices of people who follow Jesus. The salt and light do not exist just for show or self-edification—they describe action, movement, even a way of life that points to something bigger, to a *telos* or end game outside the things themselves. Considering this passage about light, Powery explains:

> In the contemporary Western/Northern world, it is difficult to imagine a world without light. When it was nightfall, in the ancient world, it was dark . . . In Jesus' usage, the light is not simply to allow others to see whatever they wish, but it is for others to witness the acts of justice that Jesus' followers perform. Beyond that, it allows the audience to recognize the cause of these actions, the God of heaven.[1]

In other words, the light is instrumental unto a particular purpose: illumination is meant to highlight and prioritize both the acts of justice and mercy and the Giver of the justice and mercy.

We work a lot as pastors and professors, leaders and practitioners to encourage others to "let their light shine," as we should. But Powery's reminder here is that the light is destined for a particular use—it is not just about illumination, or witnessing, or influencing *in general*, but that light is illuminating something bigger, broader, and something outside of ourselves. We are intended to shine light on the radical call to justice and mercy found in the beatitudes that turns things on their heads, teachings that hold up the vulnerable and weak and those thirsting after God's justice. Our light is meant to move people out of the darkness by illuminating the radical, counter-cultural, and distinct priorities of God.

In a similar trajectory, my church tradition The Evangelical Covenant Church (ECC), upholds "freedom in Christ" as one of our six core Affirmations. But the ECC speaks about freedom in a particular way—we are free from certain things, in order to be free for other things. We name freedom not just for the sake of being able to do or believe whatever we want; freedom is framed within community, within faithfulness, and within mission to say that we have freedom in non-essentials through the gifts of the Spirit in order to be united through our diversity as one Body in Christ.

"This freedom is a gift of God in Christ, and it manifests itself in a right relationship with God and others. It is not a private gift to be used selfishly, but is given to serve the community and the world. For Paul, this freedom means that we are set free from the power of those things that on their own tend to divide. United in Christ, we offer freedom to one another to differ on issues of belief or practice where the biblical and historical record seems to, we can bring our diversity of opinion, experience, ethnicities, background, and even religious practices all to the cross—and there we find our unity."[2]

1. http://www.workingpreacher.org/preaching.aspx?commentary_id=842 accessed June 1, 2015.
2. "What Does the Covenant Church Believe? A Brief Look at Covenant Affirmations." Covenant

Without erasing or talking over or whitewashing difference, this tradition works to affirm that we are free *from* the natural divisions of ethnicity, class, and gender to be free *for* each other. We are free *from* limiting ten-point doctrines to be free *for* the holistic Good News of the Bible. It is like the light that Jesus preached about—we are free *from* the darkness, not just so we ourselves can see—but because then we are free *for* others, *for* lifestyles rooted in justice and mercy, *for* a lifetime of behavior that points others toward the Source of the light, the Originator of the illumination.

"Being the light," then, is not about a quality we have to develop or keep for ourselves; it is not something to consume or get better at, nor is it an option to rest in the glowing light as a gift unto itself for those already gathered near the source. "Being the light" is not unlike the freedom found in my tradition's affirmation—it is a calling forth, an identity-shaping reality gifted from the Giver that intends and necessitates action, and that invites us and all those around us to be free from the darkness, from division, in order to be for the work of justice, and for God's presence in the world.

Illumination as Discipleship: The Invitation to Racial Reconciliation

What then does it mean to be free from the darkness in order to be the light? What does it look like to be free from division and instead be radical followers of God's justice? And what do we need to determine in order to "be the light"—on what do we shine, or give attention, or highlight through our lives? How do we know to where and to whom we are called to be the light?

One reality to which the light of Christ must be brought is the increasing scandal of racial injustice that our nation has witnessed at traumatic levels throughout 2014 and 2015. Sadly, the tragic loss of life and violent treatment of people of color, especially African-American men and women, is not new—this type of violence has a long and layered history in the U.S. But this season is almost numbing as name after name is added—names of black women and men being unjustly killed, beaten, arrested, pulled out of pools or out of their cars; as vigils, marches, hashtags and grief are continually required; as advocacy and prophetic leadership and faithful response often do not seem sufficient. The nation recently witnessed the slaughter of nine faithful leaders at their evening Bible Study at Emanuel AME Church in Charleston, South Carolina, and subsequent black churches being burned throughout the south. This horrifying death was brought directly in the name of white supremacy, even while influential voices clamored to disconnect race from the story. The brutality of racial injustice, the misinformation on so many fronts, and the pre-existing divides in our nation and in our churches can sometimes seem overwhelming in the face of this ever-growing pain and complexity. Some of us, especially those who have the option to choose, may be tempted to turn away from these discussions of racial injustice that ensue and crescendo, in order to avoid the grief and anger, guilt and fear, or simply as

Publications. Chicago, IL.

we try to cope. Others may be suffering from bone-deep weariness, a tiredness from generations upon generations who continually see the death of faces in the news who could be their sons or their uncles, their mothers or their sisters, caught on camera, reduced to a sound bite, as entire lifetimes are snuffed out. Many of us are tired, we are weary, we are confused, and we do not have practice talking about or living out racial reconciliation as part of our call to be counter-cultural followers of Christ.

There is a deep need in our country and in our congregations to address the deadly and deadening realities of racial injustices that we are living through. There is a thirst for more light, more illumination, more understanding to be shone on these places of death and fear and pain and guilt. Instead of turning away, or being influenced by the conversations the world is having around divisions and misunderstanding, as followers of Jesus we are invited to "be the light" and magnify a God who sees and provides for those who are most vulnerable, alone and without voice.

This call to be the light in places of racial injustice is not new for those who follow Jesus. The realities of race and injustice, the imbalance of power concerning who had voice or was seen, and who had political cover or protection, are all woven throughout the Scriptures. Throughout the Old and New Testaments we see how social structures and our sinful uses of power divide us from each other; it is why Jews avoided Samaritans, why there was surprise when a foreigner like Ruth was grafted into Jesus' family tree, why disbelief was expressed when an Ethiopian was among the first converts to the Christian faith. We see it in the Scripture throughout the prophets and in the teaching of Jesus, when the foreigner and the immigrant needed special protection, when unity was preached to connect slaves and free people in the early church, when the Gentile widows did not get as much food as the Jewish widows and the first deacon board was formed to ensure fair distribution. The biblical witness teaches us that Jesus followers engage in racial reconciliation, therefore, as a core part of their identity, as a way to "be the light" and counter-culturally shine attention and hope on the vulnerable, the meek, the oppressed, the over-looked and the unseen.[3] We are called to pay attention and then advocate for the people, pain, and death that the world may not have the eyes to see, because our Savior commanded us to.

Racial reconciliation is a call to deeper discipleship—no more, and no less, than part of our identity-shaping reality as followers of Jesus who are the light of the world. We cry out to the world, our nation, and the church to notice racial injustices, to better protect the vulnerable, to rightly see our history and to plan for a hopeful, more just future, because it is part of who we are. We do not engage in racial reconciliation for a political purpose, to be hip or angry, or to conserve or justify our needs, but as disciples of Christ. Just as a city on a hill shines light for miles and miles through the

3. This brief treatment obviously cannot sufficiently explore the many ways that Scripture and Christian Theology have throughout history addressed race and power; for more in depth studies on this work, see excellent work done by J. Cameron Karter, Willie Jennings, Richard Twiss, Soong-Chan Rah, Brenda Salter McNeil, James Cone, Brian Bantum, Ada Maria Isasi-Diaz, and Gustavo Gutierrez.

darkness, the church must cry out in the midst of the current confusion and pain—look, Black lives matter! Justice and mercy matter! God is the Giver of all these good gifts and God matters! Sometimes people may protest, "Why are you playing the race card?," when race is brought into the conversation, as if naming race is introducing a new concept or creating division that was not previously there. But naming racial injustice is not playing a new card—it is intentionally naming realities and principalities already at work, and inviting awareness and light to shine in that space. Naming racial injustice is asking the church to once again notice what the Scriptures and our Savior call us to see, and to shine light on that pain and suffering. Naming racial injustice is a call to confess, grieve, and mourn, and then to share the radical redemption of Christ with those who thirst for justice/righteousness.

Illumination as Transformative Hope: Be the Light

Even in the midst of so many racial injustices, death and the darkness—there are already glimmers of hope if we look closely. With the light of Christ, we can see invitations for transformative, counter-cultural, kingdom-minded conversations and faithful discipleship happening right now. Many of you as practitioners and leaders within communities and churches are at the center of these places of potential light that may shine into the brutal, burdensome heaviness of racial injustice. You are the ones who bring the hope, host the conversations, pray for healing, grieve with the mothers, phone congressmen and educate your neighbors, hold prayer services and advocate for your children. Because that is what illumination looks like next to despair—it is powerful and life-changing, like a city on a hill that can be seen for miles, witnessing to the world a distinct kind of people who live out radical commitments. Illumination is pointing people to God as the Giver of justice and then living out racial reconciliation and justice Monday through Sunday—at work, on Facebook, with your family, in the community, during worship, in multicultural settings where translators are needed, and in white monocultural spaces where sometimes race or police brutality or violence would never be brought up. Illumination holds up and draws attention to people of color who are without the choice to turn away, constantly living out this pain and under this burden, and makes space for white people or others with various degrees of racial privilege to learn, to grow, to confess, and to be part of Christ's call to discipleship together. Being the light is both a gift and a call, to be who Jesus asks us to be and to follow in the footsteps of the One who still brings light and hope to the vulnerable and the over-looked, to those whose faces are too often in the news and to those grieving in the pews, so that together we can show the world a whole other way to be.

If you are not sure what this looks like, here are some ideas of tangible practices for the church to engage in as we work to be the light, and be transformed by the light, as disciples together on this journey:

1. We pay attention and are bothered by the racial injustices rocking our nation and our churches—death, confusion, lack of protection, and injustice should call forth lament, grief, and listening, as if this death was happening in our own family. Because of course, it is; #BlackLivesMatter is a call that the larger church must hear as a reminder coming to and from within our own Body of Christ. Even if some of us we don't immediately identify with the pain of the African American community and churches suffering, our own Body was attacked in Charleston, our own family members are being targeted in church. If we do not already see the connections and the need for justice, lament, and discipleship within the Black Church's grief, we must start there. Ideas: read different news sources, develop relationships or shared services with churches in your denomination who are African American or multi-cultural, hold a lament service on Sunday morning to name and help form your congregation around the pain and death happening in the world and to break the idea that speaking about race is taboo or off limits.

2. We listen, learn, and follow local leaders—in order to see these injustices and their related spiritual dimensions. We may need to better educate ourselves on the history of our nation and the various issues related to racial injustice such as police brutality, mass incarceration, the #BlackLivesMatter movement, and other stories from various communities of color. People of color often shoulder the burden of racial injustice on their own, because being white grants the privilege of not having to name or engage race. Sometimes other communities of color are also able to sidestep issues most prevalent in the Black community, or are even pitted against the Black community—sometimes through fear around immigration, or the myth of being the "model minority." We have to be counter-cultural and listen to each other in the Body, however, especially to leaders within the communities being most grieved by the injustice. Ideas: invite a speaker from the Black Church to meet with your pastors and preach at your church, start a book series on faith and race for your church's small group ministry to learn more about race together, have regular confessions or prayer times during worship that intentionally name pursuing racial justice as an act of discipleship.

3. We acknowledge that spiritual powers and principalities are at work and that we cannot do discipleship alone—we need the power of the Holy Spirit to undergird this for the long haul, and we need community in order to stay healthy. Sometimes this means taking a break from the darkness and death, sometimes it means self-care and staying with safe people, sometimes it means challenging ourselves to engage again and show up and speak out. This work always requires relying on Christ and acknowledging that we do not know what to do apart from the guidance of the Spirit's healing, shaping, and encouraging us to receive hope as well as bring hope to the world. Ideas: pray regularly and consistently with others about racial injustice and discipleship, gather trusted friends and leaders in the church to consider how in your context you might care for those especially vulnerable and grieved by the racial injustices

occurring, hold a support group or intentional pastoral visitation to simply be present and grieve alongside those in pain and who may feel alone or not seen.

4. We remember both the personal and systemic realities at work within racial injustices—it is not simply one person or one experience, but a long history of abuses and pain that are brought up each time another death or racial injustice is leveled. Our response must be to also see the individual grief and pain involved, and to also think bigger, systemically, and with God's call to righteousness and justice in mind. Black Church folks were not only impacted by the attack at Charleston AME because of the deep grief of that community, they also knew that just as being black in that Charleston church was not safe, the same racial injustice and hate made their churches, their families, and their pastors targets in Seattle, in Chicago, in Atlanta and in L.A. When we engage individuals we do not need to argue, prove a point, or ask one person to educate or explain racial realities to us, but we pastorally and graciously come alongside. When we see these truths, then we engage the systemic realities that threaten and harm so many of those we love by speaking up, showing up, advocating, noticing our own cities and churches' level of awareness and accountability, and working to change the future. Ideas: join advocacy campaigns to speak up and write elected officials in your town or state toward better policies and laws, march or speak up online when specific policies like police brutality or sentencing laws may be impacted by public vote, organize meals or childcare to tangibly support families or friends impacted by racial injustices.

5. We accept this invitation as discipleship and remember that we bring the hope—we have access to the spiritual resources and the Body of Christ's relational resources to witness to the world a counter-cultural, radical way to live. We are free *from* the divisions of the world and the hopelessness around us, and free *for* being united in our diversity as One Body, and free *for* proclaiming the kingdom of God over all forms of death and injustice. Thankfully it is not up to us to rescue or fix someone or some system—we advocate, we love, we proclaim, we lament, and we learn because Christ calls us to follow in discipleship—no more and no less. We rest in God's ultimate provision and in the truth that together, we are transformed as we bring transformation, we experience illumination as we bring the light, and the more we see each other the more we need and may receive each other. This is not a short-term, easy, one-size-fits-all-contexts kind of work—but it is fulfilling, it is life-giving, and it requires a lifetime of following the Giver of all good gifts. Ideas: Read scripture. Commit to your local church. Invest in your community. Be the Light. Amen.

Bibliography

Covenant Publications, *What Does the Covenant Church Believe? A Brief Look at Covenant Affirmations*. Chicago, IL.

Powery, Emerson, "Commentary on Matthew 5:13-20." http://www.workingpreacher.org/preaching.aspx?commentary_id=842 (accessed June 1, 2015).

Part II

Deepening the Ministry of CCDA

JESUS' SOLIDARITY WITH THE PRISONER
A CHRISTOLOGY OF INCARCERATION AND REENTRY

ERIC HARMON

Two criminal defense attorneys chatted during lunch. Their conversation was not particularly interesting until one of them exclaimed, "Jesus, Jesus, Jesus! Everyone is trying to find Jesus! I know where to find Jesus. Jesus is in prison, because that is where all of my clients find him!" The two burst into laughter. The quick-witted comment the lawyer made about his clients was more of an unintentional deep theological observation than a joke. Jesus is in prison, and He and many of His fellow inmates who have had a meaningful experience with Him during their incarceration will be getting out soon.

The experience of incarceration is woven throughout the biblical narrative: from the first parolee Cain, to Jesus' execution between two criminals, to John's writing of Revelation while being detained. The Biblical reentry experience is understood as Israel's release from bondage and exodus from Egypt to the Promised Land. These narratives are quite familiar to the American people. These Biblical narratives are directly relevant to the statistics and realities of incarceration in the United States today.

Between the years of 1980 and 2008, state prison populations have climbed from 500,000 to more than 2.3 million.[1] After returning home from their incarceration, these citizens face collateral consequences that limit their ability to obtain employment and housing.[2] Many of these people come from the margins of society. Of the 2.3 million incarcerated over 1 million are African-American. Men and women in prison are two to four times more likely to be afflicted with serious mental illness. Between 2000 and 2009 the number of women incarcerated climbed 22%. The United

1. "Criminal Justice Fact Sheet." Criminal Justice Fact Sheet. Accessed February 11, 2015. http://www.naacp.org/pages/criminal-justice-fact-sheet.

2. Pinard, *Reflections and Perspectives on Reentry and Collateral Consequences*, 1223

States spends over 70 billion dollars annually on corrections and yet it is expected up to two-thirds will re-offend soon after their release from a correctional facility.[3]

With much of the Biblical narrative centered around characters whose stories resemble the lives of those incarcerated today, what does the Bible have to say about these issues? Where is Jesus in all of this? Where is his Church? This paper argues it is necessary to identify and understand Jesus' solidarity with the prisoner in order to render ecclesial engagement with issues of incarceration and reentry more relevant and effective. Jesus assures His solidarity with those on the margins, the "least brothers and sisters of mine." He explicitly names those in prison.[4] This low Christology of Jesus' solidarity with the prisoner gives the Church a relational and functional example of how to engage issues of incarceration and reentry. Exploring the depth of "solidarity" will provide the thread needed to weave the Christological theme throughout the theology of incarceration and reentry. Examining the Beatitudes and the Judgment Scene in Matthew 25 as an inclusion is integral to understanding Jesus' unique relationship with those incarcerated and provides a basis for incarceration theology. By applying the classic Christological principle of the interchange of properties (*communicatio idiomatum*) to the Exodus narrative, an adequate theology of incarceration and reentry can be developed. After establishing a Christological theme of solidarity throughout the incarceration and reentry experience, a reciprocal relational response is prescribed as the Church engages those in prison or reentering society.

Solidarity

The word "solidarity" is not used explicitly by Scripture to describe Jesus, but its theme is deeply infused with the purpose of His coming. Solidarity is first modeled for us for by the loving nature and mutuality present within the relationship of the Trinity. Christians are called to mirror a "Trinitarian life of self-giving" by embodying a relational solidarity between one another like Jesus did. Solidarity equips Christians to bear one another's burdens and enables them to see the "other" as a brother or sister.[5] Who is the "other"? What if it were Cain, a brother who became an "other," who committed the first capital offense and received probation instead of the death penalty? Do Christians ask themselves, "Am I my brother's keeper?" The same evil thought that prompted Cain to act is the same evil thought that resides in the heart of all of Adam and Eve's children every time they become unjustly angry.[6] While it may be a stretch for many to feel a kinship to those incarcerated, Christians' alliance to Jesus provides

3. "Reentry Facts & Trends." CSG Justice Center. Accessed March 05, 2015. http://csgjusticecenter.org/reentry/facts-trends/.

4. Matthew 25: 31–46

5. Beyer, *The Meaning of Solidarity in Catholic Social Teaching*, 16–17

6. Matthew 5: 21–22

the correlation.[7] Jesus assures his solidarity with those on the margins, the "least of these brothers and sisters of mine."

Together Christians form a collective view that goes beyond any one individual: "Solidarity also encourages mutuality because the oppressed have their own perspectives, abilities, and spiritualities to share with those who seek to empower them."[8] "Love is a reciprocal force" and requires complete giving and receiving.[9] To love is to be in solidarity, to be in solidarity is to listen, to listen is to understand, and to understand is to be equipped to act. Solidarity is the choice mode of relationship between the prisoner and the Church. It is in solidarity that both parties have the potential to be liberated. The Church has the opportunity for liberation from "ignorance about systemic issues of injustices, neglect, and abuse– injustice, neglect, and abuse that began at home and in school for the child behind the juvenile or adult inmate with whom we are talking, praying, or sharing the Eucharist."[10] The prisoner has the chance for liberation not from the accountability of fulfilling a fair and just sentence of the law, but from external oppression, for transformation, to a life of hope.[11] Liberation is found "not by sheer power and might, which Jesus intentionally avoids, but by love's vulnerable solidarity."[12] Solidarity is the choice mode of relationship because it is the same mode Jesus chose in relation to humankind when He came to announce the good news of the Kingdom of God.

Jesus' Solidarity Within Incarceration Theology

The Bible is replete with characters who have been incarcerated justly or unjustly, committed a serious criminal act worthy of imprisonment, or have been closely associated with criminals. Cain murders his brother and receives probation instead of the death penalty. Jacob is a mislabeled sex offender who saves the children of Israel by bringing them into Egypt during a time of famine. Moses, a murderer who is never brought to justice for his crime, leads the children of Israel out of Egypt when they were in bondage. David was an untouchable syndicate, yet was called "a man after God's own heart." John the Baptist was imprisoned and beheaded for speaking against moral corruption within the political system. Jesus' freedom is exchanged for that of a murderer's and is then executed as an enemy of the state between two criminals. Paul, who was deeply aware of his moral violation by persecuting the Church, is instead imprisoned for preaching the gospel. Peter has escape charges and John wrote the Book of Revelation

7. First Corinthians 7: 22

8. Beyer, *The Meaning of Solidarity in Catholic Social Teaching,* 16–17

9. O'Collins, *A Biblical, Historical, and Sytematic Study of Jesus Christ,* 311.

10. Vargas, *Who Ministers to Whom: Matthew 25: 31–46 and Prison Ministry,* 135

11. Pounder, *Prison Theology: A Theology of Liberation, Hope and Justice,* 282

12. Reynolds, *Vulnerable Communion: A Theology of Disability and Hospitality,* 229

while being detained. While the Bible has much to say about incarceration, the study of theology has not said enough equal to its place in the biblical narrative.[13]

The Church's call to be in solidarity with those in prison comes from Jesus' explicit depiction of his solidarity with the prisoner. When examining the Beatitudes and the Judgment Scene in Matthew 25: 31-46 as an *inclusio*, the call to solidarity with those in prison becomes clear.[14]

> Blessed are the poor in spirit . . . , blessed are they who mourn . . . , blessed are the meek, blessed are they who hunger and thirst for righteousness . . . , blessed are the merciful . . . , blessed are the clean of heart . . . , blessed are the peacemakers . . . , blessed are those who are persecuted for the sake of righteousness.[15]

In the Beatitudes, Jesus describes what is often understood to be human states of brokenness to be states of blessedness or states of "blessed brokenness." Those in prison are often poor in spirit and mourning. There are some who are meek, and a good many who hunger and thirst for righteousness and seek a clean heart. There are peacemakers preventing prison violence and even those persecuted for the sake of righteousness. Prison provides an environment ripe for "blessed brokenness." Jesus does not conditionally bless these states according to what a person did or did not do to find themselves in these positions. Jesus did not say "blessed are they who mourn for they will be comforted, but not they who mourn because of their own poor choices." He simply states, "blessed are they who mourn."

While Jesus' authority as the Son of God alone gives Him enough power to declare states of "blessed brokenness," He provides a better understanding of why these broken states are blessed on the other end of this *inclusio* found in the judgment scene of Matthew 25: 31–46.

> Then the king will say to those on is right. 'Come, you who are blessed by my Father. Inherit the kingdom prepared for you from the foundation of the world. For I was hungry and you gave me drink, a stranger and you welcomed me, naked and you clothed me, ill and you cared for me, in prison and you visited me.' Then the righteous will answer him When did we see you a stranger and welcome you, or naked and clothe you? When did we see you ill or in prison and visit you? And the king will say to them in reply, Amen, I say to you, whatever you did for one of the least brothers and sisters of mine, you did for me.[16]

Just as the prisoner experiences "blessed brokenness" in his condition described in the Beatitudes, so do the hungry, the thirsty, the stranger, the naked, the ill, and

13. Pounder, *Prison Theology: A Theology of Liberation, Hope and Justice*, 279

14. Vargas, *Who Ministers to Whom: Matthew 25: 31–46*, 129

15. Matthew 5: 3–10

16. Matthew 25: 34–40

all others who are just as vulnerable. These vulnerable people in a state of "blessed brokenness" are blessed because of Jesus' solidarity with them, so much so that what is done to "least brothers of mine" is considered done to Jesus himself and becomes the measure by which the nations are judged. Currently, there is no consensus among theologians concerning the message Jesus intended for the hearers of Matthew 25: 31–46; some suggest it is a call to mission, while others believe it is the hearers themselves who were being identified as the "least brother of mine."[17] Perhaps the only ones who had the faith to accept this claim of "blessed brokenness" when it was proclaimed were those who understood that the one making those claims also had the authority to offer redemptive wholeness, by not only welcoming the weak and outcast, but "also by taking on and experiencing their vulnerability directly, such that he compassionately suffers with them."[18] This news of Jesus' solidarity with the suffering is liberating and is the very basis of incarceration theology.

Jesus' Solidarity within Reentry as Understood through the Exodus Motif

While a well-developed theology of incarceration is lacking within Biblical studies, there has been even less said within the study of theology about reentry. The consideration of reentry is a necessary component of a theology of incarceration. If Jesus is in solidarity with those incarcerated, how much more after their release? Further, He is in solidarity even after as they continue to suffer despite already paying their price to society. The Exodus motif provides a framework for understanding reentry within incarceration theology. Israel's exodus from Egypt has many parallels to the experience of returning citizens, which makes it an ideal Biblical example of processing the reentry experience theologically. Of further benefit for understanding those reentering, is applying a Christological interchange of properties to the exodus motif.

> When Israel was a child, I loved him, and out of Egypt I called my son"
>
> HOSEA 11:1

The event of the Exodus is a archetypal biblical narrative that informs the beginning, middle, and end of redemptive history. Patterson and Travers note, "God initiates the New Covenant in Jesus Christ in terms of exodus motifs." All four Gospels use exodus imagery to tell the story of redemption.[19] There are many prisoners who also understand exodus as an example of redemption and speculate what their own exodus might

17 Heil, *The Double Meaning of The Narrative of Universal Judgment in Matthew 25: 31–46*, 3–4

18. Reynolds, *Vulnerable Communion: A Theology of Disability and Hospitality*, 228

19. Patterson and Travers, *Contours of the Exodus Motif in Jesus' Earthly Ministry*, 37–46.

look like.[20] A Christological interchange of properties provides a theological lens that illuminates the reentry and exodus experience as it correlates to Jesus' solidarity with the prisoner. The first interchange is the interchangeability between Jesus and Moses. While Moses is a son of Abraham leading the people of Israel out of bondage from Egypt and into the Promised Land, Jesus is often seen as a second Moses; however, Jesus is the Son of God leading all of God's people out of bondage to sin and into the Kingdom of God. The second Christological interchange is the interchangeability between Israel, called as God's son, and Jesus called by God as his own son. Exodus 4: 22 illustrates God's calling of Israel as his son: "So you will say to Pharaoh, Thus says the LORD: Israel is my son, my firstborn." In Matthew 3:17, God names Jesus as his son, "And a voice came form the heavens saying, 'This is my beloved Son, with whom I am well pleased.'" Jesus and Israel become interchangeable, perhaps suggesting Jesus' kinship with those who are in bondage. These two interchanges of properties present the Christological message that Jesus leads those who suffer out of bondage. These two Christological instances of the interchange of properties also set the stage for a set of parallels that provide the framework for what a theology of reentry might look like. A theology of incarceration and reentry embraces the story of the Exodus as a Christological model for the freeing of the oppressed.[21]

There are many parallels that can be gleaned from the Exodus and a Christological understanding of reentry. The following is a reflection upon three key themes: trust, new birth, and personal and communal accountability. The parallels between Israel's forty years in the desert, Jesus' forty days in the desert, and returning citizens under correctional supervision provide a reentry theological understanding of trust. Numbers 32: 6–13 describes a point when Israel again fails to trust that God can bring them into the land He promised them; God declares they have not followed Him "unreservedly" and as a result will wander the desert for forty years. As Jesus is in the desert for forty days, His trust in Scripture delivers him from temptation: "If you are the Son of God, tell these stones to become bread' Jesus answered, 'It is written: 'One does not live on bread alone, but by every word that come forth from the mouth of God.'"[22] Trusting God, trusting others, and trusting themselves becomes a major issue for returning citizens. It is especially difficult to trust in God's provision: how many have reoffended when they did not trust, but instead tried to turn a rock into bread? In solidarity, Jesus leads those reentering society to freedom who trust Him.

Israel's passage through the Red Sea, Jesus' example in baptism, and the returning citizen's exit from prison provide a reentry theological understanding of rebirth. Exodus 14 describes Israel's passage through the Red Sea and the destruction of Pharaoh's army, actualizing an end to their oppression and a new birth on their journey to the Promised Land. The Red Sea event is also a foreshadowing of Jesus' baptism.

20. Ekblad, *Reading the Bible with the Damned*, 97

21. Pounder, *Prison Theology: A Theology of Liberation, Hope and Justice*, 283

22. Matthew 4: 3–4

Jesus' baptism is not only reminiscent of the Red Sea event, but it also initiates his earthly ministry, proclaiming the Kingdom of God and is symbolic of his death, burial, and resurrection to come. Seventy-three percent of prison chaplains say that religious conversion is "very common" among the incarcerated and many of these people are baptized.[23] Walking out of the prison doors is much like a Red Sea experience, symbolizing an end to bondage and representative of a new life to come. While there are many who embrace this new birth, there are some who cry out with a sense of institutionalization, "Why have you led us out? Were there no beds left in prison?" and soon return. In solidarity, Jesus leads those reentering society to freedom who have embraced their new births.

The parallels between the giving of the law in Deuteronomy, Jesus' fulfillment of the law, and returning citizen's reflections upon a formative experience provide a reentry theological framework of personal and communal accountability. The Ten Commandments provides a sense of obeying God by observing personal and communal accountability. Jesus perfectly describes personal and communal accountability as He declares the greatest commandment: "Love the Lord your God with all your heart and with all your soul and with all your mind" and then further clarifies, "And the second is like it: "Love your neighbor as yourself."[24] While imprisonment alone is not enough to bring about corrected behavior, for those who do the work to reflect upon rights and wrongs done, personal and communal accountability can emerge from those who have the courage to act upon lessons learned and from what scripture teaches. In solidarity, Jesus leads those reentering society to freedom who have become personally and communally accountable.

The Church's Response as Relational and Reciprocal

Just as Jesus is in solidarity with those incarcerated and reentering society from incarceration, He calls the Church to be in solidarity with those individuals as well. There are some ministries who have heard the call yet come across as patronizing and paternalistic by refusing to recognize Jesus' solidarity with those incarcerated. They attempt to play savior to the broken by failing to engage in reciprocal ministry.[25] What kind of ministry would the Church of today provide to Dietrich Bonhoeffer, a man guilty of conspiracy to commit murder? Would they preach at Bonhoeffer, never expecting he has anything to contribute because of his incarcerated status? While the Church recognizes the depth of Bonhoeffer's theological genius as something not often seen in prison, there are those incarcerated and reentering who walk with God just as closely

23. Chaplains' Perspectives on the Religious Lives of Inmates." Pew Research Centers Religion Public Life Project RSS. March 21, 2012. Accessed March 08, 2015. http://www.pewforum.org/2012/03/22/prison-chaplains-perspectives/.

24 Matthew 22: 37–40

25. Haysom, *Prison's Door to Freedom,* 145

or maybe even closer than Bonhoeffer. What kind of ministry would the Church of today provide to Paul, a man who was never prosecuted for his most heinous acts of persecuting the Church? Instead of forever stigmatizing Paul, the Church forgave and embraced him, sending him out to do the work of God's call. Paul was eventually incarcerated: not for persecuting the Church, but for inciting riots with the Gospel! Is the Church missing out on potential Pauls because of stigmas related to past misdeeds?

A church engaging in reciprocal and relational ministry with the incarcerated or those reentering is in solidarity with those who have been imprisoned just as Jesus. There comes a sense of liberation from fear when those incarcerated engage in mutual ministry with those from the Church on the outside.[26] While there already exists a pipeline from school to prison, is it possible to imagine a pipeline from prison to pew? Many of those incarcerated and returning home feel like the Church is a place they will not be welcomed.[27] This is unfortunate, as obviously there exists a body of Christ on the "inside" just as well as on the "outside." To deny such a possibility is to limit the freeing power of Christ and is a set up for ministries to become paternalistic in nature. A Christology that acknowledges Jesus' solidarity with those incarcerated and reentering society equips the Church with the theological backing to join in solidarity and engage in holistic ministry in a relational and reciprocal way. By doing so, both parties unite and promote one another's participation, challenging individual and systematic opposition to undergo their own conversion.[28] In solidarity with one another, the incarcerated, reentering, and free Christians will bring about the Kingdom of God.

Bibliography

Beyer, Gerald J. "The Meaning of Solidarity in Catholic Social Teaching." *Political Theology* 15, no. 1 (2014): 7–25. doi:10.1179/1462317X13Z.00000000059.

"Chaplains' Perspectives on the Religious Lives of Inmates." Pew Research Centers Religion Public Life Project RSS. March 21, 2012. Accessed March 08, 2015. http://www.pewforum.org/2012/03/22/prison-chaplains-perspectives/.

"Criminal Justice Fact Sheet." Criminal Justice Fact Sheet. Accessed February 11, 2015. http://www.naacp.org/pages/criminal-justice-fact-sheet.

Ekblad, Bob. *Reading the Bible with the Damned*. Louisville, KY: Westminster John Knox Press, 2005.

Haysom, Elizabeth. "Prison's Door to Freedom." *Dialog: A Journal of Theology* 46, no. 2 (2007): 131-38. doi:10.1111/j.1540-6385.2007.00319.x.

McKinley, Rick. *Jesus in the Margins*. Sisters, Or.: Multnomah Publishers, 2005.

O'Collins, Gerald. *Christology: A Biblical, Historical, and Systematic Study of Jesus Christ*. Oxford: Oxford University Press, 1995.

Patterson, Richard D., and Michael Travers. "Contours of the Exodus Motif in Jesus' Earthly Ministry." *Westminister Theological Journal* 66 (2004): 25–47.

26. Pounder, *Prison Theology: A Theology of Liberation, Hope and Justice*, 283

27 Mickinley, *Jesus in the Margins*, 43–56

28. ibid, Beyer, *The Meaning of Solidarity in Catholic Social Teaching*, 18

Pinard, Michael. "Reflections and Perspectives on Reentry and Collateral Consequences." *The Journal of Criminal Law & Criminology* 100, no. 3 (2010): 1213–224.

Pounder, Sadie. "Prison Theology: A Theology of Liberation, Hope and Justice." *Dialog* 47, no. 3 (2008): 278–91. doi:10.1111/j.1540-6385.2008.00402.x.

"Reentry Facts & Trends." CSG Justice Center. Accessed March 05, 2015. http://csgjusticecenter.org/reentry/facts-trends/.

Reynolds, Thomas E. *Vulnerable Communion: A Theology of Disability and Hospitality*. Grand Rapids, MI: Brazos Press, 2008.

Vargas, Alicia. "Who Ministers to Whom: Matthew 25:31–46 and Prison Ministry." *Dialog* 52, no. 2 (2013): 128–37. doi:10.1111/dial.12027

Heil, J. P. "The Double Meaning of the Narrative of Universal Judgment in Matthew 25.31–46." *Journal for the Study of the New Testament* 20, no. 69 (1998): 3–4. doi:10.1177/0142064X9802006901.

IDA B. WELLS
POETIC JUSTICE

DOMINIQUE DUBOIS GILLIARD

Ida B. Wells is the most unsung freedom fighter in U.S. history. Her pursuit of justice spurred the Great Migration, halted the barbarous—nationwide—epidemic of lynching, and helped birth the NAACP. Born a slave—in Holly Springs, Mississippi—Wells overcame what seemed to be insurmountable odds to become one of the most courageous, prophetic, and influential leaders our nation has ever produced. In fact, long before Rosa Parks, Wells refused to give up her seat on a train in deference to a white patron; her case was tried in court and she initially won.[1] In spite of not being acknowledged, and remembered, for this, or many of her other accomplishments, few people have affected the history and trajectory of our nation like Wells.

When Wells was just sixteen, both of her parents and her infant brother died in the Yellow Fever Epidemic of 1878; a plague that killed over three hundred people in Holly Springs. Ida was the oldest of five remaining children (another brother died earlier of spinal meningitis) and upon her parents' death, the community decided to distribute the children to be adopted by other families. Ida, at the age of sixteen, refused to allow her family to be separated and decided to step up and shoulder the burden of caring and providing for her younger siblings. This virtuous decision dramatically altered her life, but she did not allow it to consume her.

Faced with a nearly impossible situation, Wells confronted it with fearless tenacity. In the face of the overt racism and sexism plaguing our nation in 1878, she quit school, went to work, and with no credentials provided for a family of six. It was unheard of for a woman this young, bearing so many responsibilities, to independently support a family of this size. Due to this, many people throughout the community were highly suspicious of her and her ability to make ends meet. Rumors spread about how she earned the money to support her family, and one particular instance set the

1. Not surprisingly, the case was later retried and overturned in the defendants favor.

town's gossip mill ablaze. Dr. Gray, a white physician, decided to return the savings that Wells' deceased father entrusted to him, as a way of aiding the family. Gray met Wells in the town square to return the money and when the townspeople noticed the monetary exchange, she was immediately branded a harlot and was fervently accused of prostituting herself.[2] Nevertheless, Ida used the majority of this money to enroll in Rust College and while at Russ, she got and maintained a job teaching in a rural school for three years.

When her brothers were old enough to settle into apprenticeships in carpentry, Ida took her sisters and moved to Memphis to live with her aunt. Upon arriving in Memphis, she was informed that she had to wait to take the credentialing examination for Memphis public school teachers, so in the meantime she decided to accept a teaching job in Woodstock, a rural community outside of the city. On May 4, 1884, twenty-two-year-old Ida boarded a train to Woodstock for her job. On the ride she was asked and then told by the train's conductor to move out of her first class seat in order to accommodate a White patron. Wells purchased a first-class ticket and had every right to refuse to move and she did just that. In her autobiography, Wells wrote, "I refused, saying that the forward car [the "Jim Crow car"] was a smoker, and as I was in the ladies' car, I proposed to stay . . . [The conductor] tried to drag me out of the seat, but the moment he caught hold of my arm I fastened my teeth in the back of his hand . . . He went forward and got the baggageman and another man to help him and of course they succeeded in dragging me out."[3] Wells was forcefully removed from the train and the other passengers—all whites—applauded.[4]

Seventy-one years before Rosa Parks refused to move to the back of a bus, Wells refused to acquiesce to the conductor's unjust, White supremacist order to give up her seat. Wells sued the company, using the recently passed Civil Rights Act of 1875 to win the lawsuit against the Chesapeake and Ohio Railroad in 1887. She was awarded $500 as compensation for her damage, but the Tennessee Supreme Court soon after reversed the verdict. Infuriated by the Supreme Court's decision, Wells began writing prophetic political columns highlighting injustices like the one perpetrated against her, particularly in church newspapers.

Soon after this injustice, Wells secured a job in the Memphis public schools and she used her savings to buy part ownership of a small Memphis newspaper, *Free Speech and Headlight*. During this time Wells discovered that she was being paid thirty dollars a month at her teaching job, while white teachers were being paid more than

2. Cornel West and Christa Buschendorf *Black Prophetic Fire*, (Boston, MA: Beacon Press, 2014), 140.

3. Ida B. Wells, *Crusade for Justice: The Autobiography of Ida B. Wells*, ed. Alfreda M. Duster (Chicago, IL: The University of Chicago Press, 1970), 38.

4. Lee D. Baker. "Ida B. Wells-Barnett and Her Passion for Justice." http://people.duke.edu/~ldbaker/classes/aaih/caaih/ibwells/ibwbkgrd.html.

twice her salary.[5] In 1891, Wells was fired from teaching in the Memphis school system because of a scathing article she wrote highlighting and critiquing racism, institutional injustice, and particularly the unequal funding of Black schools by the board of education. After being fired, Wells became a full-time journalist.

As a journalist, Wells frequently wrote her editorials under the pseudonym "Iola," for protection and as a way of garnering a broader readership. Within her writing she condemned lynching, violence against blacks, disfranchisement, disproportionate school funding, institutional injustice, and White supremacy. Wells said, "It was through journalism that I found the real me."[6] Wells was an investigative reporter, before this term was used. In 1892, she investigated a story which crystalized her life's calling. As Wells was beginning to make a name for herself as a prophetic voice in the city, she started investigating the tragic story of her three friends who were lynched on March 9, 1892.

Tom Moss—and two of his employees—Will Stewart and Calvin McDowell were beaten, tortured, and hung by a lynch mob in Memphis. Tom Moss, was not only a respected black store owner, but also one of Ida's best friends; she was his daughter's godmother. Ida dug deep to uncover the truth behind these murders and she ultimately discovered that her friends were murdered because of the financial success of The Peoples Grocery, Moss' store. White businessmen in Memphis were feeling the economic strain from the success of flourishing Black businesses within the Black community, dollars which White businessmen were accustomed to receiving and thus felt entitled.

Wells writes about how White lynch mobs routinely tried to conceal their true motive for lynching under the veneer of rape accusations. This allowed them to legitimate their terrorist activities by claiming to defend the virtue and purity of White women. Wells says "No nation, savage or civilized, save only the United States of America, has confessed its inability to protect its women save by hanging, shooting, and burning alleged offenders."[7] Wells is the first scholar-activist to combat the caricature of Black males as brute, rapist, preying on White women. She exposes this narrative as a farce, as a pretext for legitimating the terrorist activities of White supremacists who were hell-bent on sustaining the oppressive racial hierarchy.

Wells' writing was always bold; she routinely spoke hard words of truth to power. This case was no exception. In May of 1892, she warned Memphis' White male citizens to be careful with their terrorism and caricature of Black men:

> "Eight Negroes lynched since last issue of the Free Speech. Three were charged with killing white men and five with raping white women. Nobody in this

5. West and Buschendorf Black Prophetic Fire, (Boston, MA: Beacon Press, 2014), 146.

6. Paula Giddings, Ida: A Sword Among Lions; Ida B. Wells and the Campaign Against Lynching, (New York, NY: Harper Collins, 2009), 69.

7. Ida B. Wells-Barnett, "Lynch Law in America." The Arena 23.1 (January 1900): http://courses.washington.edu/spcmu/speeches/idabwells.htm.

> section believes the old thread-bare lie that Negro men assault white women. If Southern white men are not careful they will over-reach themselves and a conclusion will be reached which will be very damaging to the moral reputation of their women."[8]

As a consequence of exposing what she unearthed in her investigation of her friend's murder and her militant warnings to the White power structure, White elite put a bounty on her head and she was run out of town. Vigilante thugs threatened her life, destroyed her printing press, and warned her to never return to Memphis. These violent threats were meant to silence her and to suppress the truth that she excavated. Wells refused to concede to such tactics. She left Memphis, but only to continue exposing White supremacy and combating the vicious legacy of lynching nationwide. In fact, Wells' crusade against lynch law in the United States ultimately took her beyond our nation's borders. She lectured in Europe on the subject matter. Her biggest lecture tour was in Britain where she formed the British Anti-Lynching Society.

Upon being run out of Memphis, Wells accepted T. Thomas Fortune's invitation to write for his newspaper, *The New York Age*. And it was here, in New York, that she published her two seminal texts, *Southern Horrors* (1892) and *A Red Record* (1895). While in New York, Wells remained indignant about the attacks on her and the enduring presence of lynching throughout the nation. She used the power of the press to fight back, imploring Black residents of Memphis, and the South at large, to leave the South for the safer alternative, the North. Wells said "The people must know before they can act, and there is no educator to compare with the press."[9] While in New York, Wells became more aware that lynching was a nationwide problem and she decided to make a career of investigating and writing lynching exposés. Wells wrote, "Our country's national crime is lynching. It is not the creature of an hour, the sudden outburst of uncontrolled fury, or the unspeakable brutality of an insane mob."[10] Wells became intent upon mobilizing a movement committed to end this social ill, by any means necessary.

In 1893, Wells moved to Chicago. Wells was the first Black correspondent to be paid to write for a mainstream White newspaper, the *Daily Inter-Ocean*.[11] Her first major story in Chicago exposed the ban on African-American exhibitors at the 1893 World's Columbian Exposition. Wells composed and circulated a pamphlet entitled "The Reason Why the Colored American Is Not in the World's Columbian Exposition." In Chicago, Wells continued to lead the anti-lynching campaign and began to

8. Ida B. Wells, *Crusade for Justice: The Autobiography of Ida B. Wells*, ed. Alfreda M. Duster, (Chicago, IL: University of Chicago Press, 1970), 65-66.

9. Ida B. Wells-Barnett, *Selected Works of Ida B. Wells-Barnett*, (New York, NY: Oxford University Press, 1991), 42.

10. Ida B. Wells-Barnett, "Lynch Law in America." http://courses.washington.edu/spcmu/speeches/idabwells.htm.

11. Ibid, 147.

further expand her work into broader issues of segregation and in support of women's suffrage. Her activism helped to prevent the establishment of segregated schools in Chicago and in 1986 she joined W. E. B. Du Bois to work in the Niagara Movement, which advocated for the full civil rights for blacks. In 1909, Wells-Barnett helped Du Bois and others form the National Association for the Advancement of Colored People and in 1913 she founded the Alpha Suffrage Club of Chicago, the first black suffrage organization. In 1930, she ran for the Illinois legislature, becoming one of the first black women to run for public office. A year later, in 1931, she died at the age of sixty-nine. Wells' legacy and fearless activism was venerated in 1990 by the nation with the Ida B. Wells Commemorative Stamp.

The Emergence of Lynch Law

The lynching era is an extremely unnerving period within our nation's history. Due in large part to Wells, we know that during a fifty-year period of time ranging from 1890 to 1940, approximately 5,500 African Americans were documented as lynch victims.[12] Lynching reached its peak in 1892 shortly after Reconstruction ended. We should not take that to mean that lynchings became rare after 1892.[13] In fact, in Phillips County Arkansas 237 Black people were lynched in 1919 during the Elaine race riot.[14] Due to realities such as this, the lynching era became known as the "Nadir Period,"[15] the lowest period of U.S. race relations. While Blacks were not the exclusive victims of lynchings, they were without question the primary prey of this form of vigilante "justice."[16]

It is also important to note that lynching was not a problem prior to emancipation. Wells explains, "In slave times the Negro was kept subservient and submissive by the frequent and severity of scourging, but, with freedom, a new system of intimidation came into vogue; the Negro was not only whipped and scourged, he was killed."[17] Because, as the following quote from historian Jaqueline Royster indicates, slaves were simply too profitable to kill:

12. Rayford Logan. *The Negro in American Life and Thought: The Nadir, 1877-1901,* (New York, NY: Dial Press, 1954), 23.

13. "How Did Black Women in the NAACP Promote the Dyer Anti-Lynching Bill, 1918-1923?" http://womhist.alexanderstreet.com/lynch/intro.htm.

14. "Map of 73 Years of Lynchings," http://www.nytimes.com/interactive/2015/02/10/us/map-of-73-years-of-lynching.html.

15. Nadir means the lowest point; time of greatest depression. For U.S. race relations, this period of time following Reconstruction is identified as the era where racism was worse than any other period in our postbellum nation. This phrase was coined by Rayford Logan.

16. Ken Gonzales-Day, *Lynching in the West, 1850-1935,* (Durham, North Carolina; Duke University Press, 2006). This book details how in California, Latino/as–particularly Mexicans–were the primary victims of lynching, but the book also states that a few African Americans, 41 Native Americans, & 29 Chinese immigrants were lynched in California during this period of time.

17. Ida B. Wells. "Southern Horrors: Lynch Law in All Its Phases," in *Southern Horrors and Other Writings: The Anti lynching Campaign of Ida B. Wells, 1892-1900* (Boston, MA: Bedford/St. Martin's, 1997), 1.

> The lynching of slaves was rare, first and foremost because it would result in a loss of property and profit. Obviously, it was more profitable to sell slaves than to kill them. Second, there were more advantages to planters when slaves were executed within the law, as planters were compensated for their lost "property." Third, the lynching of slaves served to undermine the power base of the South's wealthy, white, landowning aristocracy. In effect, mob violence against slaves would have transferred the power of life and death from the hands of planters to the hands of the mob, whose numbers were quite likely to include non-elite whites, as well. Such a transfer of power would have loosened the systems of control, the general stronghold of the landed aristocrat over both economic and political life. The lynching of African Americans before the Civil War, therefore, was exceptional indeed.[18]

During the Nadir Period, the practice of lynching became so commonplace that the Tuskegee Institute, a predominately black institution in Alabama which later became Tuskegee University, decided in 1881 to begin issuing annual reports on lynchings occurring nationwide. Astonishingly, it was not until 1952 that the institution was able to report a year where there were no lynchings nationwide.

While popular belief still holds that lynchings only occurred in the South, this is not true. Lynching was a national sin; the South alone cannot be condemned for this grotesque practice. While it is true that lynching was particularly prevalent in the South, it was not exclusively a Southern horror. Lynchings were enacted as far North as Minnesota and Illinois, and as far West as California and Oregon. In fact, one of the largest spectacle lynchings to ever occur took place in Duluth Minnesota in 1920, where some accounts say as many as 10,000 people served as spectators at this lynching.[19] Moreover, this was not an anomaly for the North. We see virtually the same exact thing ten years later in Marion, Indiana, on August 7th 1930. Reports estimate that as many as 15,000 people gathered at this lynching to watch two African American teenagers be tortured, mutilated, and ultimately executed.[20] In both cases, African American men were killed for allegedly raping white women.

Lynchings were routinely photographed and turned into postcards, which would then be used to promote future lynchings.[21] According to historian Ralph Ginzberg, "lynching [which also frequently included burning, castrating, & disfiguring the victim,] were spectacles, announced in advance, attended by Whites, including women and children, and covered on assignment by newspaper reporters in a manner not un-

18. Jacqueline Jones Royster. *Southern Horrors and Other Writings: The Anti-lynching Campaign of Ida B. Wells, 1892-1900,* (Boston and New York: Bedford/St. Martin's, 1997), 8.

19. "The Lynchings." Minnesota Historical Society. http://collections.mnhs.org/duluthlynchings/html/lynchings.htm.

20. Fran Kaplan. "An Iconic Lynching in the North." http://abhmuseum.org/2012/01/an-iconic-lynching-in-the-north/.

21. James Allen. Without Sanctuary: Lynching Photography in America. http://withoutsanctuary.org/.

like contemporary coverage of sporting events."[22] People would send these postcards to their friends inviting them to attend upcoming lynchings as if these executions were some sort of theatre at a local country club. Wells also wrote that "the nineteenth century lynching mob cuts off ears, toes, and fingers, strips off flesh, and distributes portions of the body as souvenirs among the crowd." The most disturbing part about this is that people who self-identified as Christians played a significant role in these events, in both the promotion and execution of lynchings.

Furthermore, it was normative for infants and children to be taken by their parents and grandparents to see these "spectacle" lynchings. This was an intergenerational sin! Imagine the psychological trauma of growing up seeing this sort of dehumanization on a semi-regular basis. This had to profoundly impact these young minds. Being taken to public executions, where Blacks were looked upon as a kind of game animal to be caught and executed for pleasure, had to permanently hallmark the image of Black inferiority within the young, impressionable, minds of White children. This does not even begin to address the catastrophic psychological effects this had to have on the entire African American community, who saw family members, friends, and neighbors persecuted with such brutality.

Dr. Cornel West says that "Ida B. Wells is not only unique, but she is the exemplary figure full of prophetic fire in the face of American terrorism, which is American Jim Crow and Jane Crow, when lynching occurred every two and a half days for over fifty years in America."[23] West goes on to say that Wells was the sole African American leader of her era's acclaimed leaders, male or female, who used her voice to prophetically galvanize the masses against this atrocity and sacrificed her social stature and popularity in order to speak truth to power. West says,

> Du Bois, who did want to talk about civil rights, who did want to talk about political rights, but in no way targeted the lynching face of American terrorism the way Ida B. Wells did. Ida B. Wells, in so many ways, teaches us something that we rarely want to acknowledge: that the Black freedom movement has always been an anti-terrorist movement, that Black people in America had a choice between creating a Black al-Qaeda or a movement like Ida B. Wells', which was going to call into question the bestiality and barbarity and brutality of Jim Crow and American terrorism and lynching, but would do it in the name of something that provided a higher moral ground and a higher spiritual ground given her Christian faith, not opting for a Black al-Qaeda.[24]

West is correct in naming lynching as American terrorism. West states that "when people think of terrorism, they usually think of . . . Islamic brothers and sisters,

22. Ralph Ginzberg, *100 Years of Lynching*, (New York, NY: Lancer publishing: 1962), 46. Lynching frequently included ritualized burning at the stake, castration, and mutilation in addition to the victim being hung from a tree.

23. West and Buschendorf *Black Prophetic Fire*, (Boston, MA: Beacon Press, 2014), 140.

24. Ibid, 141.

whereas, of course, terrorism has been integral to . . . the American democratic experiment, beginning with indigenous peoples and slavery. But after the Civil War, we get a new form of terrorism . . . that sits at the center of American life, and Ida B. Wells forces us to come to terms with that."[25]

In the midst of what may be a new Nadir of race relations in our nation, we have a lot to learn from Ida B. Wells. She uncompromisingly spoke truth to power and almost singlehandedly exposed the horrors of lynching. Today we find ourselves in a similar predicament as Wells did, but it remains to be seen if we will face it with the same integrity, tenacity, and fortitude which she embodied. Recent studies reveal that Black males are at a 21 times greater risk of being killed by police officers during encounters with them, than are their White counterparts.[26] Moreover, it has also been found that in seventeen of the largest American cities, police killed Black men at higher rates than the total U.S. murder rate in 2014.[27] Furthermore, in the 365 days following the killing of Michael Brown, 314 more Black Americans reportedly lost their lives during interactions with law enforcement.[28] This problem is not restricted to Black men. Black women and transgendered individuals are amongst the re-crucified masses too. In the face of such despair, let us look to the life, legacy, and witness of Ida B. Wells as an exemplar of faith expressing itself in love, of placing the needs of others before our own, and bearing witness to the truth of the Gospel in the face of death!

Bibliography

Allen, James. *Without Sanctuary: Lynching Photography in America*. Internet. Available from http://withoutsanctuary.org/.

Buffalo and Erie County Historical Society, "How Did Black Women in the NAACP Promote the Dyer Anti-Lynching Bill, 1918-1923?" I University of Arizona, May, 2002. Internet. Available from http://womhist.alexanderstreet.com/lynch/intro.htm.

Equal Justice Initiative, "Map of 73 Years of Lynchings," The New York Times, February. 9, 2015. Internet. Available from http://www.nytimes.com/interactive/2015/02/10/us/map-of-73-years-of-lynching.html.

Gabrielson, Ryan., Ryann Grochowski Jones and Eric Sagara "Deadly Force, in Black and White." *ProPublica: Journalism in the Public Interest*, October 10, 2014. Internet. Available from http://www.propublica.org/article/deadly-force-in-black-and-white.

Giddings, Paula. *Ida: A Sword Among Lions; Ida B. Wells and the Campaign Against Lynching*. New York, NY: Harper Collins, 2009.

25. Cornel West and Christa Buschendorf. "Cornel West on What the Courageous Ida B. Wells Taught Us About the Black Freedom Movement A look at the willingness of this young, militant, uncompromising, bold, and fearless woman and journalist." Alternet, Beacon Press, September 30, 2014. http://www.alternet.org/books/cornel-west-what-courageous-ida-b-wells-taught-us-about-black-freedom-movement.

26. Ryan Gabrielson, Ryann Grochowski Jones and Eric Sagara "Deadly Force, in Black and White." http://www.propublica.org/article/deadly-force-in-black-and-white.

27. "Mapping Police Violence," The National Police Violence Map. http://mappingpoliceviolence.org/

28. Ibid.

Ginzberg, Ralph. *100 Years of Lynching*. New York, NY: Lancer publishing: 1962.

Gonzales-Day, Ken. *Lynching in the West, 1850-1935*. Durham, North Carolina; Duke University Press, 2006.

Kaplan, Fran. "An Iconic Lynching in the North," America's Black Holocaust Museum. August 2012. Internet. Available from http://abhmuseum.org/2012/01/an-iconic-lynching-in-the-north/.

Logan, Rayford. *The Negro in American Life and Thought: The Nadir, 1877-1901*. New York, NY: Dial Press, 1954.

Lee D. Baker. "Ida B. Wells-Barnett and Her Passion for Justice." April 1996. Internet. Available from http://people.duke.edu/~ldbaker/classes/aaih/caaih/ibwells/ibwbkgrd.html.

Royster, Jacqueline Jones. *Southern Horrors and Other Writings: The Anti-lynching Campaign of Ida B. Wells, 1892-1900*. Boston and New York: Bedford/St. Martin's, 1997.

Wells, Ida B. *Crusade for Justice: The Autobiography of Ida B. Wells*. Ed. by Alfreda M. Duster. Chicago, IL: The University of Chicago Press, 1970.

Wells-Barnett, Ida B. "Lynch Law in America," The Arena 23.1 (January 1900): http://courses.washington.edu/spcmu/speeches/idabwells.htm.

Wells-Barnett, Ida B. *Selected Works of Ida B. Wells-Barnett*. New York, NY: Oxford University Press, 1991.

Wells, Ida B. "Southern Horrors: Lynch Law in All Its Phases," in *Southern Horrors and Other Writings: The Anti lynching Campaign of Ida B. Wells, 1892-1900*. Boston, MA: Bedford/St. Martin's, 1997.

West, Cornel and Christa Buschendorf. *Black Prophetic Fire*. Boston, MA: Beacon Press, 2014.

West, Cornel and Christa Buschendorf. "Cornel West on What the Courageous Ida B. Wells Taught Us About the Black Freedom Movement A look at the willingness of this young, militant, uncompromising, bold, and fearless woman and journalist." Alternet, Beacon Press, September 30, 2014. Internet. Available from http://www.alternet.org/books/cornel-west-what-courageous-ida-b-wells-taught-us-about-black-freedom-movement.

"The Lynchings." Minnesota Historical Society. Internet. Available from http://collections.mnhs.org/duluthlynchings/html/lynchings.htm.

"Mapping Police Violence," The National Police Violence Map. Internet. Available from http://mappingpoliceviolence.org/

FROM FERGUSON TO MEMPHIS
THEOLOGICAL REFLECTION AND ENGAGED PRAXIS

ANDRE E. JOHNSON

Theological reflection, according to Kathleen McAlpin, "is a way of doing theology that starts from the experiences of life and leads to searching in faith, for deeper meaning, and for the living God." [1] The goal of such reflection is to determine how one should live his or her life differently as a result of how their faith or spiritual practice has influenced their decision making. While theological reflection centers on the practitioner's experiences regarding faith, it does not work in isolation. Theological reflection places the "reflector in conversation with other sources of the revelation of God, primarily the faith tradition of the person or community." [2]

Typically, when students of theology speak of reflection, they do so in the classroom, through reading—whether devotionals, spiritual journals or writing abstract reflections often devoid of contextual realities. However, from my personal perspective, theological reflection goes much deeper than simple classroom analysis. Theological reflection does not happen in a vacuum—it arises out of a specific context. In theological reflection, one engages and participates in culture and society with an eye towards reflecting at a deeper level. The person doing the reflection—or the reflector, can have epiphanies or experiences of enlightenment. When writing these reflections, many times they are thick with descriptions of personal, interpersonal and intrapersonal experience. Moreover, theological reflection, when produced publically, has the potential to reach broad audiences and may help to lead to individual and social change. When made public through "witnessing" or the "testimonial," the reflection not only can lead to personal and social change, but the hope of more holistic transformation, first within the individual and then more broadly within society.

1. Kathleen, Alpin. *Ministry That Transforms: A Contemplative Process of Theological Reflection*, Liturgical Press Collegeville, Minnesota. 2009, 7

2. Kathleen, Alpin. *Ministry That Transforms: A Contemplative Process of Theological Reflection*, Liturgical Press Collegeville, Minnesota. 2009, 7

In January 2015, I took a class of Memphis Theological Seminary students to Ferguson, Missouri for a one-week immersion class. The class consisted of predominately Christian pastors, church leaders, and lay members who represented multiple denominations and various theological perspectives. This essay aims to provide my personal theological reflection as I share my own experience in putting together and being a part of this immersion class. Second, some of the students in the class reflect on their experiences. Finally, this essay outlines how some of the students are moving from theological reflection to concrete praxis here in Memphis, Tennessee.

Instructor Reflection

For Memphis Theological Seminary's January term, I decided to offer our Urban Theology class. Typically, classes in urban theology explore and focus on the current dynamics found in urban society that call and challenge the church to re-examine methologies of ministry. In addition, urban theology allows students to examine their own theological positions as they specifically relate to urban situations of poverty, addiction, racism, sexism, violence, unemployment, environmental toxicity, prison, and inadequate education. Drawing from their particular ministry location and realizing that any authentic theology must be contextual, I expected students to examine their own theological positions through the contextual lens of the Ferguson fiasco. In this class, we examined how an urban theology could speak to the events and happenings in Ferguson. Additionally, we examined how people constructed the "sacred" in all that occurred in the aftermath of Michael Brown's death. While I thought the context would provide for a good class, there still seemed to be something missing.

Then it hit me—we needed to be in Ferguson. In other words, this class needed to be an immersion experience. We needed to get out of the classroom and experience—as much as possible, the sights, sounds, and situations that make up Ferguson. We needed to listen to protesters and activists. We needed conversations with pastors and church leaders who have been ministering in this situation. We needed to see the place where Darren Wilson shot and killed Mike Brown. We needed to see the burned and boarded up buildings. We needed to talk with people tear gassed and shot with "rubber bullets" by law enforcement officials. We needed to listen to guest speakers who would come to and give us testimony. We needed to stand with those who stand in the street and experience life through their eyes. We needed to see how people are coming together and standing with each other against all odds. We needed to see how those who protest still find time to relax, have fun, and enjoy each other's company. We needed to see this and much more if this class was to be meaningful for any of us. Collaborating with Webster Groves of Eden Theological Seminary in St. Louis and their academic dean Deb Krause, we made plans to head to Ferguson. Little did I know how much impact this class would have on my own personal ministry. Little did I know how much this class would (re)shape my theology. Little did I know how much this class would reorient my teaching. Little did I know how much transformation was about to happen.

Student Reflections[3]

Many of the students had profound transformational experiences. One first-year seminary student felt a call to go to Ferguson before the class even began. The class gave this student an opportunity:

> Early on in the process before learning about and actually enrolling in the class, I wanted to come to Ferguson. Something inside of me kept tugging at me, saying get to Ferguson. I am still not sure yet why coming to Ferguson had such an overwhelming urgency for me. I felt called to go . . ..I had a natural curiosity about what was happening here and I preferred to "see for myself," but more so than that I felt the *spirit beckoning me to come.*

Another student, though excited about the class and the opportunity to go to Ferguson, did not know what to expect. "Before leaving for Ferguson," the student wrote, "I didn't know what to expect. I didn't know if the 'movement' was just hype or something truly organic. From the evening I got there, I realized the latter was true. I learned that the Spirit is truly alive and well."

One student had a healthy suspicion of well-meaning whites who were part of the movement. The student reflected:

> My first impression was that of another well-meaning white person who wanted to say they helped. Then [this person] will go back to life as usual with no real accomplishments other than feeling better. However, after observing [some] for a while, I no longer hold this opinion. Some appear genuinely to care for people and the people of this struggle. [They have] been in the trenches working for the betterment of humanity and community and has done it quietly in a support role.

Another student, in noting white clergy's presence in the movement wrote:

> I paid close attention to the involvement on behalf white clergy. It was good to see that we have at least reached the point in history where this would be more expected. We saw in the film "Selma" how diverse groups of clergy came to support the cause of the Civil Rights Movement. And we were able to be a part of and see how some of the same interactions and involvement was taking place in Ferguson not only on a mass movement level in terms of protesting but now we see it moving forward in terms of political and social language that can be used in the rebuilding of the old and constructing of new possibilities for citizens of Ferguson and abroad.

3. Student reflections are from their final reflection papers in class. Used with permission.

The young people in the movement impressed my students. However, one student offered a word of caution in reflecting about the youth and their role:

> One thing I was glad to keep hearing is that this was truly a movement of the young people and that they had the respect of key clergy and community activists and leaders. I personally find this to be a blessing and a curse. Often times when one is given a large amount of power or responsibility, then it gets polluted quickly and can end up doing more harm than good. I think it is good that the young people have power and the ability to organize and maneuver, but as I tell my young people as often as possible, if you have no identity or history and spiritual core, than any movement will be as one built upon the sand that all though breathtaking and beautiful, is washed away with the shifting shore.

For many students, the immersion trip offered them a chance to reflect on their own ministries. Noting many of the students currently served as pastors and/or other church leaders, the immersion trip to Ferguson had them reevaluating what they would do when they returned back to their respective parishes. One student wrote:

> The events in Ferguson have lit a fire in me from which I must light flames of justice in my own lane. I serve as a youth director at my home church. Part of my ministry is teaching the young people ages 11-17 years old. Part of our education will now be rooted in a more historical perspective. Looking at the cradle to grave prison pipeline in connection with spiritual identity and servant leadership, my attention has been directed to the juvenile justice system in regards to Memphis and how young black males especially, are unfairly targeted and convicted of crimes that do nothing but further push them into a system that is set up to make it as difficult as possible for them to reach legitimate success.

Yet another student examined and reflected on what it meant to be a Black Christian in the movement. Upon returning home to the congregation, transformation had taken place while in Ferguson.

> For me, the Movement has shed light on the theme of purpose. Upon returning to Memphis, I was able to speak with the young people at the church about finding their meaning and purpose in life. Using what I learned from Ferguson, I explained to them the importance for the young Black Christian to not only keep the Bible [close] but [also] to understand their history in order that they may begin living their lives as if they themselves are making history.

Still another student noticed through all of the frustration and ill treatment many residents of Ferguson and the Greater St. Louis County were getting, many of them still had hope:

> There were a variety of perspectives on the movement taking place in St. Louis and beyond, with some tension mixed into the conversation, yet their greater purpose was to fight for justice for all people. They hoped that their efforts would produce meaningful and purposeful results and for many of them it seems as if that hope comes from their faith.

Further, the student noted that some people in the streets did not ground this hope in an understanding of hope from a "Christian" perspective:

> [I]t was quite evident that a hopeful people were leading the efforts to raise awareness about a flawed system and were working together to break down that system. As people of the Christian faith we live our lives hoping for something greater, a kingdom experience on earth and in heaven, and do so much of what we do to help others experience that as well. The efforts of the people leading the movement in Ferguson may not explicitly have this as their guiding force, but they work toward a kingdom experience as I see it. They're fighting for a greater life for all people, especially for the marginalized and oppressed.

However, some challenged this notion of hope and replaced it with something else. In reflecting on time spent with activists, some had a healthy disdain for the church. One student wrote how many expressed their frustrations with the church. In reflecting on one activist in particular, this student wrote, "[The activist] honestly spoke about the hopelessness that he experiences and the absence of God that he feels at times when participating in the movement. 'Why put my trust in a church and god that is not present in the midst of the turmoil that is taking place?'" Further, this same student wrote about pain and rejection from others:

> We heard his cries of pain for people that are not experiencing life in the ways in which they deserve. We heard the pain and frustration from a college student who saw no need for the church as she knew it because it did nothing for her that was good and only seemed to reject her and her friends because of who they were.

This activists' hope came from the "community that she was now part of in the fight for justice and change." The student continued to reflect about this female activist:

> She saw hope in the people who loved all, without the exclusion she had felt from the church, and had found a community of people who were working together for the good of humankind. She chuckled when we asked if she was hopeful and responded by basically say, "Why would I do this if I didn't hope something good would come from it?" She had found her "church" with the people of the movement; they loved each other and were fighting for the oppressed and marginalized. It didn't come in the form of traditional Christian

> faith but in many ways they are following the ways of Christ in much of what they do. Their actions show their hope.

Another student reflected about seeing the memorial site dedicated to Mike Brown:

> Pulling up to the site it took me a few minutes to take in the surroundings and gathering my bearings as I pieced together what that scene must have been like on the day the Mike Brown was killed in the street. The stuffed animals, signs, and pictures, which had been left to memorialize Brown, are the first things that I noticed when pulling up to the apartment complex. They cover the road and yard where the killing took place and serve as a constant reminder of what took place that day in August. . . . .We attempted to process something that had once been so distant to us and reduced to videos and pictures in the mainstream media. It was now at our feet and we were standing in the thick of it.

As the course instructor, I wanted to provide the students with hands-on opportunities to engage and take action. Part of our experience in Ferguson was a direct action we took in shutting down traffic on I-70. This came as a surprise for all involved and was not part of the syllabus! About that experience, one student wrote:

> Our excitement was faced with the reality of actually joining with the brothers and sisters in Ferguson, our new friends, to stand in the street for 4.5 minutes in memory of Mike Brown to send a message that the systems are broken. After hearing from Rev. Renita the difference between being an ally and living in solidarity with the people of the movement, we knew that being an ally was no longer an option, we needed to join. My heart and mind were racing as I tried to figure out what was really going to happen. I just put my name on a list in case I get arrested and now I'm trying to process what I am about to do. Deep down I knew that this was part of the journey that I was on but it was difficult to think about actually participating in something like blocking an intersection with a group of people. Though the nerves didn't quite go away I knew what we all were participating in was the right thing and it was serving a meaningful purpose.

What really moved this student was when we started chanting and singing together as one:

> Once we began to chant together a variety of phrases there was something that moved within me, and many others, as it seemed to breathe life into something more spiritual. We were joined together with one voice in a worshipful call and response as we stopped the movement of the roads to be still for a moment and aware of injustice. A shift occurred for me as the movement we had been talking about and hearing stories about was brought to life. I saw what was taking place and I felt it within me.

Another part of our experience was to attend a poetry slam featuring the great Saul Williams. Writing about this experience, a student reflected on the spirituality of our time together:

> The messages of the poets were profound and moving as they energized the crowd and called us into greater action. In many ways, it felt like an underground rally to energize the troops and to nourish us with fun. It was a perfect way to cap off the week because of the hope that it once again offered. For people on the outside looking in all of this movement may appear disorganized, violent, or out of control but it is far from that. I see the hope that exists within the people leading these efforts in St. Louis and I see the passion they feel about justice for all people. There is a spirit that is moving within this greater movement and for a person of Christian faith it could very well be the Spirit of God. God is definitely present in this movement, even though many may not recognize it.

Engaged Praxis: Implementation of What We learned

Our trip to Ferguson was transformative for many of us. When I returned to the church I serve—Gifts of Life Ministries, we quickly instituted regular Town Hall meetings with the express purpose of presenting, discussing, and dialoguing about issues and concerns germane to our community. During one of the first town halls, I invited some of the students from our Ferguson trip to share about their experiences in Ferguson and also to talk about how the trip has shaped the futures of their ministries. Since that time, we have had other town hall gatherings discussing race, policing, education and other issues facing our community. It was the Ferguson reflections that helped us understand that communication with, not only elected officials, but also with other members in our community is important to creating the shalom that we seek.

Upon returning home from Ferguson, students incorporated what they discerned and learned into their ministries. James Carter, who serves as Youth Director at Springhill Baptist Church in Memphis, took three things away from his Ferguson experience. First, he wrote how he now understands the "value and importance of working closely with organizations committed to peace and justice and how they may serve as a resource for education and practice." This led him to collaborate with the Mid-South Peace and Justice Center in Memphis. The center bills itself as a "multi-issue, multi-race organization whose mission is to engage, organize, and mobilize communities to realize social justice through nonviolent action."[4] Additionally, the center works to "educate and train new community leaders to lead campaigns for racial, economic, environmental and social justice."[5]

4. http://midsouthpeace.org/

5. Ibid.

Second, through his experience in Ferguson, and working with the Mid-South Peace and Justice Center, Carter understands the importance of teaching youth to know their basic rights and how to handle incidents with local law enforcement. Carter's church is in a neighborhood where youth are constantly facing suspicion and often times, harassment from law enforcement. In addition, using the non-violent strategies employed from the Mid-South Peace and Justice Center, Carter teaches youth how to handle other types of confrontations youth may face.

Third, through his experience in Ferguson, Carter saw how youth needed spaces and opportunities for empowerment where their voices could be heard and respected. Moreover, he saw the need for youth to participate in artistic expression designed for spiritual growth and development. This led to two changes in his ministry. First, Carter revamped the youth Bible Study. Still grounded in the Biblical witness, Carter's Bible studies now center more on expressions and questions from youth. Second, this revelation led him to create *Inspiring Dreams*—a ministry that engages youth in artistic expression and performance. Through *Inspiring Dreams*, Carter put together art exhibits, hosted panel discussions on hip hop and the church, and formed other working relationships with Bridges and Memphis United. The ministry is now in talks with Memphis Theological Seminary and other churches in the area to plan the first Hip Hop Social Justice Conference in Memphis.

Not all the students who went to Ferguson are church leaders. Some, like Katherine Whitfield, are not members of a local church. Nonetheless, Katherine continues to feel a deep spiritual connection out of her Ferguson experience. Working at a children's hospital in Memphis, Whitfield writes: " [my] job affords me the opportunity to work with children and families who have been made poor and are among the marginalized in our community."[6] Her Ferguson experience better equipped her with "background knowledge about what many of our patients and families are facing on a daily basis."[7] While her ministry does not "take place in a traditional church setting," Whitfield believes she is given a chance to "minister both to those who seek care at this hospital and to those who provide said care."[8] She is indeed grateful for the opportunity to "learn and share stories, and to be reminded that there is a place for anger, and that sometimes the best thing I can do to show my support is to listen to someone and take steps to meet them where they are."[9]

This listening and sharing led Whitfield into some deep theological reflection. In a moving four-part essay on the *Rhetoric Race and Religion* blog, Whitfield called for an understanding of the Black Lives Matter (BLM) Movement as the new *ekklesia* or church. Whitfield sees her "church community" as those who participate in the Black Lives Matter movement. She writes about BLM:

6. Student reflection from final reflection papers in class. Used with permission.

7. Ibid.

8. Ibid.

9. Ibid.

> They are the Ekklesia—a spiritual personhood bound together in love, free flowing, informal, and assembled for the purpose of proclaiming and acting out one simple, undeniable element of Gospel truth. They proclaim that the lives of black men, women, and children *matter*, and that the age of shalom will never truly come until this truth is acknowledged and reflected in the deepest threads of our nation's social fabric.

She argues that the "ekklesia is happening all around us, and church is taking place far beyond the walls of the formal building with the steeple." Whitfield writes about how she has found her "authentic, beloved community of worshippers." and for her, they are the "ekklesia—and they have a story to tell, to any who will listen and believe."[10]

Conclusion

I have found this piercing question regarding a practical theological method very prescient: "what if we could reclaim the project of theological reflection as something that has been fundamental to the evolution of Christian thought and tradition from the very beginning? One thing we would understand is that 'theological inquiry would be seen as something generated by problematics, dilemmas, contexts and practical tasks.'"[11]

When Ferguson erupted on our television screens and social media feeds, many church leaders were not prepared. We quickly realized many who were protesting did not have a relationship with the church. Christian moralism and respectability politics did not move them. While some of us had, in the past, engaged with urban and youth ministry, we were still ill-prepared to understand the deeply embedded systems of abuse pervading in Ferguson. Civil Rights leaders, who have led movements in the past, could not get a handle on Ferguson. Even churches with a record of social justice and committed people working within those ministries of justice, found language hard to come by in explaining what happened in Ferguson.

However, what churches really began to see was Ferguson did not only happen in Ferguson. Many church leaders began to hear from their own congregation about abuses going on within their own cities—Memphis was not an exception. With the nation's high poverty rate, policing tactics, fines and abuses funding the criminal justice system and our inability to talk about race in healthy and empowering ways, many only believe it is a matter of time before Memphis is the next Ferguson—the next Baltimore—the next Cleveland.

10. Katherine Whitfield. The Church and the #BlackLivesMovement. Rhetoric race and Religion blog. Pt. 4.

11. Elaine Graham, Heather Walton, and Frances Ward. Theological Reflections: Methods SCM Press. 2005, 8

This is exactly why we need spiritual leaders who have done the theological inquiry within these specific contexts. Prior to my trip to Ferguson, someone asked me my plan for when arrived. I simply answered, "I have no agenda in Ferguson other than to listen, learn and see where God has already been working." This has been my agenda in any context and I hope it remains the agenda of my students as well. [12]

Bibliography

Alpin, Kathleen. *Ministry That Transforms: A Contemplative Process of Theological Reflection*, Liturgical Press. Collegeville, Minnesota. 2009.

Graham, Elaine, Heather Walton and Frances Ward. Theological Reflections: Methods. SCM Press. 2005

Whitfield, Katherine. The Church and the #BlackLivesMatter Movement. Rhetoric Race and Religion (blog). http://www.patheos.com/blogs/rhetoricraceandreligion/2015/05/the-church-and-the-blacklivesmatter-movement-pt-4.html.

12. *I would like to thank the Urban Theology class at Memphis Theological Seminary for their participation. I also like to thank in particular students James Carter and Katherine Whitfield for allowing me to share their work in the Memphis community.*

WHAT ARE ALL THOSE WOMEN OF COLOR DOING IN THAT ROOM?
REFLECTIONS FROM THE RAINBOW

CHANEQUA WALKER-BARNES, OLUWATOMISIN OREDEIN, ANA YELSI SANCHEZ, GINNY GILES, & SANDRA VAN OPSTAL

Christian Community Development Association (CCDA) has long recognized the experience of Christian community development is not "one size fits all." Over the years, the authors of this article have each provided workshops and retreats for CCDA specific to certain populations, including singles, married couples, parents, women, and people of color. This year, as leaders and women, we are responding to the need for culturally safe space among women of color in justice ministry by hosting a post-conference retreat where indigenous, Black, Latina, Asian-American/ Pacific Islander, and multiracial women can receive support and sustenance for our journeys. The retreat itself is racially and gender restrictive, but we believe its aims will benefit the cause of Christian social justice broadly. We invite our sisters and our brothers of all races to support us through prayer and by reaching out to the women of color in your own communities who may be in need of this unique fellowship. Because, more than you might know, many of us have considered quitting when the isolation gets to be *enuf*.

In this article, we offer reflections from women of diverse racial/ethnic backgrounds who are engaged in Christian community development and social justice ministry. Each of us, from our distinct cultural and geographical perspectives, gives voice to the unique challenges we face at the intersection of race and gender. We try to articulate the need for this retreat, for a culturally safe space. Oluwatomisin Oredein, a Nigerian American, narrates the constant state of grief many people of African descent have been embodying in the wake of repeated incidents of anti-Black police violence. AnaYelsi Velasco-Sanchez, a Venezuelan American, and Chanequa Walker-Barnes, an African American, describe how spiritual and psychological safety often elude women of color who worship and labor in Christian congregations and social justice organizations. Ginny Giles shares the perspective of a white sister-sojourner who both supports and slightly envies the idea of women of color gathering in a space that is not open to white women. Sandra Van Opstal, Latina American, tells how, despite the ways in which we are disregarded and disrespected, women of color remain devoted to serving in evangelical churches and organizations as agents of God's mission of reconciliation.

Black Fatigue, White Empathy, and the Funeral (Oluwatomisin Oredein)

As a Nigerian woman, I have had to explain to my white friends why the murders of countless black persons by law enforcement (including the justice system) and vigilantes affects me so much: personally, physically, emotionally, psychologically and spiritually. I can be a confusing case of blackness. I am not African American, but my ethnicity does not offer protection from the way people associate with me because of the color of my skin. I occupy the endangered ontology of being black.

Many white persons in my life do not know what to do with the brutality and murders, so they lament in private and say nothing to me. Some do the best they can and try to mourn and lament with me through conversation, prayer, and whatever presence they can offer. And though it is comforting, I do not know if they realize what black deaths mean to black people—they don't know how to—unless it, in some way, implicates them.

I try to explain the emotional landscape of being black today by asking my white friends and acquaintances to imagine the following scenario as literally as possible: Imagine that every black person killed by the police or vigilante is a relative of mine. Whether close or distant, we are in some way related. Every time they are murdered or die mysteriously, a funeral happens, an emotional or psychological funeral. I have the choice to attend or not, but I am fully aware that a family member has died. I may or may not have known the family member well. The person killed could be a distant relative whom I had never even met or someone very close to me. Whether they are near or far, whether I attend or not, every death warrants a funeral. I feel and know the loss.

As my friend, regardless of if you and I are close or if we are just acquaintances, you would also know about each of these funerals and you would offer me your deepest condolences. You feel the weight of my sadness, frustration, despair, and loss because you care about me. Funerals are heavy moments; when they hit me, they hit you in some way. Our relationship creates the opportunity for you to hold some of my pain.

Now fast-forward one week. Do you realize over the course of the past week you've offered condolences to me five times? Fast-forward to the end of the month.

Now the number has climbed to 20 or 30. Being there for me has made you tired. It is a lot of energy and work for you. Offering this much condolence is taking a toll on you; you begin to wonder and finally begin to understand in your emotional being that all of these deaths mean something is deeply wrong—and further, it is literally affecting the lives of all black people.

Tap into your emotional fatigue and stay there. What does it feel like to have offered condolences 30 times this past month? Sit with that. Do not try to create a solution or response. Just sit in your fatigue and understand it as a gateway to my own pain. From there, I will tell you when we are both ready to do something about the number of these deaths.

Brown Girl Worshipping (AnaYelsi Velasco-Sanchez)

"Absolute hospitality would in no way amount to the absence of violence. To the contrary, it would enthrone violence precisely under the guise of nonviolence because it would leave the violators unchanged and the consequences of violence unremedied."

—MIROSLAV VOLF

It's exhausting to be the brown girl at church.

The evangelical church.
The progressive church.
The non-denominational church.
Seemingly, any church.

I've spent 13 years volleying between these church traditions, bobbing and weaving but never quite being able to avoid the race-based offenses.

Each of us carries our own stories of what Protestant theologian Miroslav Volf would call "exclusion and embrace." This includes white people and people of color alike. The commonality ends there. Our world is run by systems that sanction racism and those systems favor white people over people of color. Rather than being a prophetic voice for the redemption or dismantling of such systems, the Church is often guilty of participating in them and perpetuating them. There are the overt acts: genocide, displacement, and colonization of the "other" in Christ's name. More common, and more insidious, are the unintentional microaggressions: the brief verbal and behavioral indignities to which marginalized people are regularly subjected. Intentional or not, they communicate the internalized biases of those in power, and Christians, including advocates for social justice, are often the perpetrators.

Since becoming a Christian, I have lived in five cities, in three different states, and worked for six Christian ministries and social justice organizations. With each has come the familiar coded language and well-meaning ignorance.

My current church is a non-denominational community that prides itself on being a multi-racial and multi-cultural space dedicated to racial reconciliation but not necessarily to racial justice. Like many well-meaning Christian entities, we often make the misstep of focusing on the cosmetic rather than the painful but necessary internal reconstruction.

My name is unique to white ears and awkward on white tongues. I get that. I know it takes a few tries before you're going to get the pronunciation right. I know you'll want to know the origins. But there are ways you ask and there are ways you don't. When I began attending my church, the following was one of my first interactions with two white women.

Woman #1: What's your name?

Me: AnaYelsi

Woman #2: So what is that? Where are you from?

Me: It's Venezuelan

Both: OMG!! Do you know [names another Venezuelan]?! She goes to our church too!

Me: No

Woman #1: Are you sure? She's Venezuelan too!

Me: [blank stare]

Both: [speaking over one another as they attempt to share a wealth of unsolicited information about my fellow Venezuelan]

There's no malice here. They want to connect. I'm the "other" and they want to find a way to build a bridge between us. Assuming I know every Venezuelan within a five-mile radius is probably not the ideal way to go about that. Perhaps a simple, "That's beautiful. Were you named after someone?" This gives me the opportunity to decide if and when I want to share my story.

We rarely discuss racism in the church. It's the sin we're too afraid to name and are ill-equipped to face. We even go so far as to lie, seeing an environment fraught with uncontested acts of racism and naming it "peaceful." When the acts are identified for what they are, we call those brave (often lone) voices "divisive." We value a "comfortable" Sunday morning over a "just" one. But whose comfort are we ensuring?

I certainly wasn't comfortable when a white Christian heard me casually slip into another vernacular while speaking on the phone to a fellow person of color and proceeded to ask me why I was "talking Black." I was far from comfortable when another white Christian who worked for the sheriff's office sat in my own living room and defended racial profiling by telling me, "You have to admit, AnaYelsi, it's people who look like you that commit most crimes anyway." I felt anything but comfortable when a white Christian and I were serving together overseas and, upon seeing my natural hair, he exclaimed, "Whoa! You look so primitive. Like one of these natives." His observation was met with hearty laughter from our entire team.

Comfortable isn't how I would describe the hurt I felt when a white Christian love interest told me, "I've thought about it [dating me] but I just don't see myself with an 'Hispanic.'" (He clarified that white-passing people were okay). I'm never comfortable when people ask my name and I have to deny my heritage by saying "Ana" instead of "AnaYelsi" because I'm tired of the conversation that will inevitably follow. I'm not even comfortable as I write this. I'm worried I've said "white" too many times and white readers will feel attacked. When do we [people of color] get a turn at being "comfortable?"

> *"For He himself is our peace, who has made the two one and has destroyed the barrier, the dividing wall of hostility, . . . His purpose was to create in Himself one new man out of the two, thus making peace, and in this one body to reconcile both of them to God through the cross, by which He put to death their hostility." (Eph. 2:14-16, NIV)*

We need to begin having conversations in the Church that will show we value the dignity of all over the comfort of the few. Our justice-seekers and peacemakers must recognize, silence in the face of racial injustice means culpability. We must ensure the consequences of violence are not ignored. This means challenging one another when we commit the "small" transgressions and it means being willing to be challenged. Those "small" acts don't feel so small to the person subjected to them. Not when they are one in a sea of many. I know I'm welcome in my church and in my organization. I'm even warmly embraced, but every one of the above stories is still an act of violence. They are wounds I carry with me. The Church can and should be an instrument of reconciliation, but we risk hypocrisy if we preach to the world but do not practice what we preach within our very own walls.

The Church and Christian movements for justice cannot continue to allow the burden to be on people of color. We're not here to be teachers or guides. We're not responsible for another's awakening to the need for racial equity. A true commitment to racial justice is taking ownership of one's own education. It's reading books by persons of colors and diverse cultural perspectives, finding answers to questions, and living in a posture of humility and learning. First and foremost, it is entering into a season of repentance and lament. I'm much more inclined to come alongside you in these efforts than I am to do the work of dragging you, unwillingly, behind me.

Is There No Place for Us? (Chanequa Walker-Barnes)

The large, flat package was sitting in the front entryway when I returned home after three days away at an evangelical social justice conference. The return address listed

"S. Gay" as the sender. It was a minute or two before I remembered placing the order. It was a print by a local artist, Shanequa Gay. I had learned of her work several months earlier, intrigued by this talented woman who shared my name.

I had ordered the print a week before the conference as an act of retail therapy. My spirit had been battered by a series of encounters with white (and often male) privilege. Three years of living, working, and worshipping in contexts where I was the only woman of color (or one of a few) had taken its toll. For the first time in my racial reconciliation journey, I did not have a culturally safe space—an environment where I was surrounded by other people of color, where I did not have to carry the burden of representation alone.

I was tired of constantly being the "yes, but . . ." voice, the sole person providing an alternative perspective in rooms where people tended to look and think similarly. I was tired of constantly being in teaching mode, explaining how the world looks differently through the lenses of race and/or gender. And, I was especially tired of being overextended by leadership roles and committee appointments that come with the territory when you fulfill multiple diversity checkboxes. It was a deep fatigue, one that seemed to emanate from my very soul.

Gay's painting, "Reverence," had spoken to my *Blackwomanweary* soul. There was something inspiring in her depiction of five Black women arrayed in white and blue, bent down toward the ground with hands on hips. It evoked sass and sisterhood and love of God's creation. Five Black women gazing downward, reverently, as if to say, "Our God is not way off in heaven somewhere. Our God is right here in this patch of ground." It seemed as though they were turning upside down the Gospel account of the woman with the hemorrhage (Luke 8:43-48). It was as if they were saying, "We may be bent, but not because we're broken."

Ironically, the conference had left many women of color bent and maybe even a little broken. The event had been a paradox of the promise and challenges of justice in Christian community. The organizers had gathered an impressive array of female leaders in racial and gender justice. One panel session featured Native-, Asian-, Latina-, and African-American women talking about racial reconciliation, a rare occurrence on a topic that is usually dominated by white and black men.

But many of the names of the women of color had been omitted from the conference brochure and website. My name was included in a few obscure places, but incorrectly. As the conference unfolded, it became clear that women of color were almost exclusively featured as panelists, their wisdom reduced to sound bites. It became even clearer, we were not the audience many of the speakers - including both white women and men of color - had in mind. On multiple occasions, we bristled at offensive comments and jokes made from the main stage, while white brothers and sisters surrounding us cheered. At one point, even the call to prayer left us stumped about how we could participate. In a room filled with over two thousand Christians who cared about justice, we were not only a minority, we were culturally and theologically isolated.

To be a woman of color committed to racial reconciliation and social justice in the Christian church—whether evangelical or mainline—is to be a perpetual outsider. While we share many of the same concerns and experiences as our white sisters and our brothers of color, our existence at the intersection of race and gender brings unique experiences. Those experiences provide a unique vantage point from which to view the complex dynamics through which race, gender, class, power, privilege, and oppression operate. But they also predispose us to unique hardships in the struggle for justice in Christian community, hardships that make us want to quit, to walk away, and to give up on the hope for beloved community.

If any of us were looking for a culturally safe space, we didn't find it in that auditorium. We found it instead on Twitter, as we began to carry on a separate, online conversation in reaction to what we were hearing. We found it in the lobby as we shared glances of recognition with women of color whom we didn't know and hugs with those whom we did. We found it over shared meals, as we vented and processed and laughed and prayed together. By the end of the weekend, we were like the women in Gay's painting, standing together in defiance and in hope, knowing that our ability to sustain the journey is borne not only by our baptism, but also of our sisterhood.

Cheering from the Sidelines (Ginny Giles)

My first thought when I heard about a CCDA retreat for women of color was "Oh cool! We need that." As a proud member of the CCDA family it seems to me we spend a lot of time teaching white people why racial reconciliation matters and how to do it. This is good. For me, the work of racial reconciliation has been my best experience with Jesus. I have personally and professionally flourished among this family of people who are willing to honestly push me to grow, as well as love me along the way. But all this growth is about me—a white woman. It's about my learning, my privilege, my "sacrifice." There is something missing when the lens of racial reconciliation is focused on white people.

Racial reconciliation is hard, hard work for people of color. We white folks rely on the people of color around us to teach us, challenge us, and soothe us when we feel guilty. We praise ourselves for attending diverse churches, but forget people of color are also giving up some of their historical expressions of worship to be a part of our diverse church. Let's be honest, we assume they are grateful for the work we are doing and rarely give a thought to the work they are doing.

This retreat is an extremely unique opportunity for women of color who are living daily lives of racial reconciliation to come together. My hope is that my beloved CCDA sisters of color will have a time to be refreshed, encouraged, and renewed for our ministries. I hope the intimacy of shared history will create a safe place of peace and calm. I hope the boundaries of African American, Latina, Asian, and Native American will be crossed. I hope this retreat will influence our entire CCDA family to be more honoring of the gifts, struggles, and successes of our sisters of color.

My second thought when I heard about the retreat was "Oh bummer, I can't go." Some of my favorite people in the world will be at this retreat and I know it is going to be a crazy good time. I sincerely hate the idea of people having fun without me. It would be easy to feel jealous, resentful, or excluded. But this is not the time for that. This is the time to be happy for the sisters who work side by side with us. This is the time to praise God for bringing this special CCDA family together. This is the time to be glad that something great is being offered for the women we love. I am excited to see how God will be honored by this gathering.

Indebted, Disregarded, Disrespected & Devoted (Sandra Van Opstal)

Indebted

In my faith journey, I thank God for the places where I can go to journey with other women in Christian leadership. These cohorts and learning communities within InterVarsity Christian Fellowship, The Evangelical Covenant, and others were invaluable to me as a young minister navigating mostly male leadership in local churches and ministries. Hallelujah and Praise God -for real- that He also provided spaces to journey as a person of color in the church. Blogs, conferences, and gatherings within the Christian Community Development Association, La Fe (Latino Fellowship), and more sustained me as I built bridges between communities in the multicultural/reconciliation/justice movement over the past two decades.

As thankful as I am for what I had, I can say that there have been VERY FEW, if any, spaces and places where I could journey my leadership as BOTH a woman and person of color: a Woman of Color. The intersection of the two has been the place with the most distinct set of questions, frustrations, and longings that had often made me feel isolated in my experiences of being disregarded and disrespected.

Disregarded

I regularly see conferences and articles that feature Christian pastors/leaders of color who "should be listened to" by the majority church (read: white pastors/leaders) and much to my continued disappointment those list rarely if ever have women on them. Why no ladies? Are women not leaders or pastors? Are we not good influencers for the Church? Do the men of color notice our absence? Do they not understand the distinct voice we bring?

Recently, a friend commented on such a list, asking, "Where are all the ladies?" to which the author replied with another post of female bloggers we need to read.

Why did his list of all women bloggers promote they were female, but his list of pastors/leaders neglected to mention they were all male? This is one example of a constant experience of being qualified and/or disregarded. And it's exhausting. Women in my community are the ones that are leading the charge for housing, immigration, and equitable education. They are the executive directors of non-profits and community mobilizers, but in the "in gathering" of clergy we are more likely to be asked for coffee then for a sermon. We have creative solutions and thoughtful reflections to contribute, but our contributions are often overlooked. I wish we had more partnership with men (including men of color) in how to increase awareness on this issue and bring our voices to the table. Our journey is distinct and one they can't fully represent.

Disrespected

Working with pastors from different denominations, cultures, and countries is a part of my ministry context. In corporate gatherings, I anticipate there will be various views on the roles of women within the church. At a recent experience, though, I left with my mouth hanging open. I was the leader of a program committee making decisions for a mission/justice related conference. At the planning meetings I repeatedly heard participants say "the pastor wants this" or "the pastor thinks that." Each time I heard this I asked, "Which pastor?" Despite being the leader, and also the pastor of a church, it was clear preference was being given to the desires of a particular male pastor of color. The constant sidelining of my thoughts, ideas, and perspectives left me exhausted by the "collaboration."

Devoted

Despite experiences like these, women of color remain committed to justice, reconciliation, and the rest of the work of the Gospel all over the world. May our eyes be opened in our contexts to see where voices are being ignored, our sisters of color are sidelined, and how the work of God can flourish when "all are welcome to the table."

Part III

Book Reviews

Prophetic Lament: A Call for Justice in Troubled Times, by Soong-Chan Rah. Downers Grove: IVP Books, 2015. 224 pages. Reviewed by M. Daniel Carroll R. (Rodas).

It is rare to find a book that weds a deep passion for an authentic and relevant Christian faith with careful attention to the biblical text. Soong-Chan Rah, Milton B. Engebretson Professor of Church Growth and Evangelism at North Park Seminary in Chicago, has provided just that with this unique commentary on the book of Lamentations. Dr. Rah is well informed about church history and modern sociocultural realities, as well as about academic studies on Lamentations and relevant ancient Near Eastern literature. This volume is an impressive work that moves comfortably between the disaster of the fall of Jerusalem in the sixth century B.C.E. and the tragedies of modern society.

Prophetic Lament is part of the Resonate series, which has as its goal that "each author approaches the subject matter not from the standpoint of detached observer but rather as a fully engaged participant in the text" (Paul Louis Metzger, Executive Editor, from the Series Introduction). Soong-Chan Rah is well placed for this task, as anyone who knows the passion of his teaching, ministry, and writing (such as *The Next Evangelicalism: Freeing the Church from Western Cultural Captivity* and *Forgive Us: Confessions of a Compromised Faith)* is well aware.

The Introduction bemoans the absence of a theology of lament and the inability to voice suffering within a North American church that has been compromised by a theology of celebration and cultural accommodation. The fourteen chapters that follow plunge head on into Lamentations in order to redirect an understanding of life and mission toward a set of beliefs, emotions, and actions appropriate to urban ministry, social justice, and racial reconciliation. Each set of chapters that comment on each of the chapters in Lamentations is prefaced by a brief reflection that serves to orient the treatment of the biblical text that follows.

An autobiographical sketch of personal and familial tragedy introduces the three chapters on Lamentations 1 and signals that we are to read about loss and sadness. The biblical exposition begins with an account of Babylon's defeat of Judah and highlights the terrible suffering in the aftermath of its siege and destruction of Jerusalem. It was impossible for the survivors to ignore the catastrophe of their experiences in the war. How different, our author points out, from many North American Christians, who either do not engage the problems of society or embrace the siren calls of a message acclimatized to the culture. What Lamentations offers us, he says, is permission to mourn and the demand that we listen to the painful stories of racial minorities. The theology of sin and guilt in this biblical book is complex: Judah had suffered due to its rebellion against God, but now the people were suffering physically and emotionally because of their present condition. Out of this agony and shame arose this insistent lament (so powerful in Lamentations as a female voice); realism had bred honest articulation of their feelings to God and neighbor, not the vacuous and irrelevant triumphalism so common in our day.

The four chapters that comment on Lamentations 2 are preceded by a story of Dr. Rah's frustration at a large pastoral conference, whose ideology championed optimism and success. Lamentations presents a very different kind of narrative, an uneasy counter-narrative of soulful wrestling with the judgment at the hands of God. Is there a lesson here for the North American church from that prophetic mourning of long ago, which recognized the guilt of disobedience and admitted the senseless pride of exceptionalism? The author describes the abandonment and demise of America's cities and the subsequent focus of many churches on Anglo suburban mores and dreams. What are ignored are powerful expressions of Christian faithfulness and ministry in urban areas among the disadvantaged and marginalized. Lamentations also has hints of hope. Then, as now, from the lives of hurting communities surfaces a trust in God to empower and restore the broken.

Three chapters are dedicated to Lamentations 3. The opening reflection probes the relationship between expressions of worship and the social contexts of congregations. How to coordinate in faithful fashion liturgies of celebration and suffering, and of spontaneity and historical resonance? The exposition of Lamentations 3 begins with an explanation of its literary form, an acrostic that utilizes the entire Hebrew alphabet. This is the longest chapter of Lamentations, and its breadth of poetic expression allows for a complete communication of emotions, which is at once aesthetically beautiful and theologically powerful. It ranges from the experience of suffering and confession to speaking of patience and hope in the sovereignty of God. In Lamentations 3 the prophet shares his own story, but it is intertwined with that of his community. This decision to identify with the transgressions and plight of his people is a model for modern-day advocates.

Lamentations 4 rehearses many of the themes of the preceding three chapters in the form of a communal lament. The prophet decries with what Jerusalem had grown comfortable and what it respected. What would he say today? Dr. Rah picks up that mantle to critique the 'dehumanization,' 'commodification,' and commercialization of evangelicalism. Ironically, these cancerous trends even have crept into the new interest in justice among younger evangelicals. Lamentations 4 exposes the shallowness of such values and unmasks the pervasiveness of sin in all persons and communities.

As in the case of Lamentations 4, there are two chapters dedicated to the exposition and contextualization of Lamentations 5. This closing chapter of Lamentations again articulates the loss bemoaned by the people of Jerusalem and their heartfelt appeal to God to remember them and to restore their fortunes and their relationship with him. This final lament and plea prompt Dr. Rah to underscore that our Christology must be characterized by lament as well as praise and that incarnational ministry requires transparent and honest living with the needy. Jesus is the One, who can respond to the anguish of Jerusalem and the modern city, but it must never be forgotten that he is both resurrected Savior and suffering Servant.

The Conclusion of *Prophetic Lament* turns to the German martyr Dietrich Bonhoeffer for an exemplar of forsaking nationalistic exceptionalism and the embrace of sacrificial service and lament. An Epilogue follows, which reflects on the death of Michael Brown in Ferguson, Missouri (August 9, 2014). This event serves as a contemporary call to mourn. As with the deaths in fallen Jerusalem, a dead body reminds us that suffering continues and that there are no easy analyses or answers. The Epilogue ends creatively with a lament for this country based on Lamentations 5.

This brief summary cannot do justice to the scope of the author's connections between the biblical text and the situation of the church, particularly in the United States. He draws from the experiences of Jews, African-Americans, Native Americans, Asian-Americans, Africans, Filipinos, and others. His comments often are deeply personal and sharp, but they also are timely and valid. *Prophetic Lament* at times is repetitive and meandering in its reflections, but that feature actually mirrors the book of Lamentations itself, which keeps coming back to the same questions and repeating the same painful sentiments. This is the way of lament: cyclical groaning, recurring doubts, intermittent moments of trust, and a hope against all hope in the dark night of a community's soul.

Soong-Chan Rah's willingness to face the issues of judgment and sin and not take the road most travelled of a tidy victimization is to be applauded. This is something that needs continued consideration. Society and its ills are complicated and multi-layered. How to sort out that confusing reality of God within life and history is the quandary of theology, the stuff of worship, the challenge of ministry, and the pilgrimage of faith. *Prophetic Lament* is a helpful resource in that rich, and sometimes painful, journey.

Where the Cross Meets the Street: What Happens to the Neighborhood When God is at the Center, by Noel Castellanos. Downers Grove: IVP Books, 2015. 183 pages. Reviewed by Zakiya Jackson.

Noel Castellanos' recently published *Where the Cross Meets the Street* provides theological recognition for a multitude of Christians and would-be believers of Christ. For much of Church history, far too many Christians have not been recognized for their *Imago Dei*. They are told, directly and indirectly, "Christ does not look like you. Christ does not reflect anything about you and your culture." The whitewashing of Jesus is unacceptable not as a judgement of whiteness but rather as a historical inaccuracy that has fostered oppressive strongholds over the collective Church for people of all ethnicities and colors. The refusal to acknowledge a revolutionary ethnic minority Jesus has crippled the ability of the Church to do what Christ did consistently—remain relevant to a hurting world. We serve a Jesus who did not need cultural assimilation, blonde hair or permission to be angry and throw things. The vanquishing of this Jesus has caused it to be unnatural for the cross to meet the streets—and in contrast Noel powerfully tells us about the harmony of this incarnational Savior.

Where the Cross Meets the Streets is a teaching narrative and testimony by Noel that utilizes scripture, poetic rhythms, and various forms of imagery to unpack an incarnational understanding of the gospel. He demonstrates that a dedication to those on the margins is central to the gospel and must be grounded in four things: proclamation and formation, the demonstration of compassion, restoration and development, and the confrontation of injustice.

There's something magnificently powerful about recognition. It is restorative, healing and empowering. It can take one from isolation to a warm, familiar embrace. And recognition is inherent to the nature of God. Again and again, Jesus acknowledges and welcomes those he encounters—to richer and fuller lives with him. Though not about the African American experience, I felt recognized as I read this book. I was recognized in Noel's Mexican American journey from southern Texas to Northern California to La Villita in Chicago. I saw a piece of myself in Noel's heart to see Mexican and Latino communities on the margins flourish. I'm grateful for what I learned about the origins of Mexican devotion to Guadalupe and how it reflects the importance of incarnational living and about Latino liberation theologians that radically changed his understanding of faith. I was connected to those stories as a fellow believer and activist because Noel welcomed me into the realities of his barrio. *Where the Cross Meets the Streets* offers affirmation for any Christian who has wondered: does Christ look like and identify with me and my cultural, ethnic identity?

There was one aspect of the book that gave me pause. CCDA continues to grow in the affirmation and recognition of female leaders. Symbolically I was concerned that only men endorsed Noel's book. I was confident that the absence of endorsements by women did not accurately reflect Noel's respect and value for women. When I contacted him with my concern, Noel responded quickly with humility and his own dismay about the absence of female leader endorsements. He explained that the endorsement process happened when he was away on sabbatical and that he was working to fix the situation for the next printing. I share this not to overemphasize an honest mistake. Rather, this oversight actually reinforces Noel's emphasis on recognition as a material commitment, and not only an academic one.

Dear White Christians: For Those Still Longing for Racial Reconciliation, by Jennifer Harvey. Grand Rapids: Eerdmans, 2014. 262 pages. Reviewed by Brandon Wrencher.

Dear White Christians is one of the most significant recent books on anti-racism and religion. As part of the Prophetic Christianity series which seeks to explore "the complex relationship between Christian doctrine and contemporary life" with the goal of "embracing shalom justice," the book exposes the blind spots of popular reconciliation and diversity frameworks for ministry. Author Jennifer Harvey deconstructs reconciliation as a paradigm and offers a constructive practical vision of reparations. Harvey is well equipped to offer such critical analysis and vision. Her PhD is from Union Theological Seminary and she has served in a host of ministry settings addressing racial justice for nearly two decades as an ordained American Baptist minister. She is associate professor of religion at Drake University. Harvey has done her work and training trying to make sense out of her own embodied white racial identity. And though the book's title would seem to limit its audience to white Christians, Harvey draws on Black studies and addresses a host of racial justice issues, so this book is relevant for an intercultural audience.

Harvey's thesis is clear: reconciliation has failed as a paradigm to address race and racial injustice in America. The Church needs a paradigm shift to a reparations paradigm to better address our racial situation. The book's primary audience is equally clear: prophetic evangelicals and mainline Protestants, especially those who are white, as the groups that are most deeply captive to the reconciliation paradigm. Harvey cites many CCDA luminaries as examples. She locates the heart of the reconciliation paradigm in the oft-repeated Martin Luther King Jr. adage that eleven o'clock on Sunday morning is the most segregated hour of the week. In this paradigm racial separation denotes racism. Racial diversity and togetherness become the primary criteria for determining racial righteousness. The question of whether the solution to our longings for diversity should come from white Christians joining ethnic minority churches is rarely given serious consideration. Issues related to structural justice are significant within visions of reconciliation but they take a backseat to the ultimate concern of inclusion. Harvey often asks students the question: what would be the difference in their responses to seeing a group of African American students walking across campus, carrying signs that stated "Black is Beautiful" versus white students carrying signs that stated "White Is Beautiful"? Almost universally Harvey's students have a positive and supportive response for African American students, interpreting this as a demonstration of community pride. But the students respond with discomfort and disapproval of such an activity among white students. This exercise exposes the incoherence of our visions of reconciliation-as-diversity. Our racial identities are not parallel. Focusing on differences may be significant in a reconciliation paradigm, but it doesn't clearly challenge us to focus on what our differences represent "on the ground." A reconciliation vision fails to emphasize that we may all need to do racial work, but we do it differently, based on particular histories and material conditions. For white folks this means that there's no way to address their racial identity apart from white supremacy. White racial identity is a moral crisis.

Reconciliation is dead, Harvey argues next. She invites us to put a moratorium on reconciliation-talk. Reconciliation is largely a one-sided white vision for white churches to become diverse by bringing more ethnic minorities to *their* churches. Rarely, if ever, is this articulated the other way around. The reconciliation paradigm assumes that to reach its vision of togetherness all races have the same ethical responsibility in cultivating trust. This grossly distorts power dynamics. To show that hers is a balanced and sober critique, Harvey shows that some versions of reconciliation do address the structural dimensions of racism. For example, though Jonathan Wilson-Hartgrove of the Rutba House demonstrates an explicit commitment to a reconciliation-diversity vision, he also contends with whiteness through his long-standing commitment to attend and serve in a historic black Baptist church in his neighborhood. But Jonathan's example is exceptional, according to sage of the movement David Janzen. New monastics are more concerned with the lack of diversity within their intentional communities. This continued lament instead of strongly encouraging examples like Jonathan's to be the norm, shows that a latent reparations paradigm is at work. Reconciliation talk cloaks and thwarts reparations work from thriving thus reinforcing barriers to authentic reconciliation. I highlight her example of new monastic communities given their traction in CCDA. Harvey credits John Perkins for having one of the more consistent visions of reconciliation. Within the three R's, reconciliation is only possible to the extent that relocation and redistribution of wealth are realized. She argues that the first step toward true racial justice is for the white church to extend apologies. Not only through word. There must be apologies in the form of material repair and persistent strategies for interrupting the structural oppression of ethnic minorities.

Harvey situates a reparations paradigm in The Black Power Movement of the late 60's and 70's, a movement radically embraced by much of the black church at the time, contrary to popular opinion. This movement said "no" to integration and diversity visions, since segregation and togetherness were not the real issues of the "color line" in America. Power was the problem, white power, white supremacy. The Black Manifesto, the Black Power movement's guiding document, demanded that power be returned to black people through very specific economic and political reparations for slavery before any talk of togetherness could be trusted or meaningful. The historical import of The Black Manifesto was overwhelmingly rejected by white Christians because of its direct confrontation to white privilege. Harvey contends that a return to this historical period is the key to unlocking a more racially just future. Her reparations vision entails: 1) making explicit the historical and material conditions on which our racial differences are made intelligible (slavery, the Middle passage, black resiliency, white terrorism, etc.), and 2) establishment of full Black empowerment through transfer of wealth and political power to Blacks from whites, without patronage, charity or pity. A reparations paradigm is only perceived as unreasonable, angry, or callous if one believes that white people do not owe Black people in this country. Harvey argues that white Christians' failure to remember Black Power as part of civil rights history is evidence of their captivity to a white supremacist reconciliation vision.

Harvey seeks to disrupt white supremacy at its roots. She asks this question: "What was so powerful that it would cause white institutions to imperil so much of what they claimed to stand for and so many of the relationships with folks with whom they insisted they wanted to stand?" (132). Answer: whiteness. Harvey defines whiteness as the "particular problem of white people's unique relationship as perpetrators and beneficiaries to supremacist racial structures . . .[and] it is also larger and more powerful than the individual white person, having taken on a life of its own . . . regardless of one's beliefs, commitments, and . . . actions, white people cannot simply 'opt out' of whiteness" (134-5). And what is so dangerous about white supremacy is the way in which it can be rendered invisible when white people are silent about or trivialize whiteness. A universalist ethic which undergirds the reconciliation paradigm also contributes to this disappearing act of whiteness by not demanding an account of whiteness. A reparations paradigm requires not only naming of whiteness but demands white moral agency through repair, redress, and repentance.

Harvey gives the reparations paradigm contemporary practical relevance. She contends that the reparations paradigm has a broad relevance beyond black-white racial issues, able to scaffold in order to address issues in diverse settings of racial injustice. Harvey applies the paradigm to diverse issues: environmental racism and land-rights struggles among Native Americans, immigration, and mass incarceration. Different racial groups or diverse groups can do racial justice work on systems and environments immediately, right where they are without having to wait for token others to show up. Harvey is careful to note that she is not advocating a separationist model, only that the urgency of anti-racism work requires we mobilize with folks where we are, always open to racial others who may join later. This especially takes away the common excuse of white folks to be silent or uninvolved on racial justice matters because persons of color are not leading or present. Harvey challenges white folks in monoracial settings to get to work focusing on structures of systemic racism right where they are even while they should be aware of justice work happening among racially diverse groups in order to strengthen anti-racism efforts. The constructionism that informs a reparations paradigm gives white people and all races, though differently, the possibility to reconstruct racial identities to be just and righteous, but not without incredible work.

Since 2000, several mainline denominations have passed resolutions and/or created committees or commissions that study whiteness and reparations. Harvey does not suggest these movements were ideal. She seeks to make these movements visible to make the reparations paradigm more real for the Church, showing significant features worth emulating and to avoid. She especially focuses on her interviews and investigation of the Episcopal Church's more sustained and ongoing reparations work through the Maryland Reparations Task Force and similar efforts in New York. Here she is honest about some of the challenges to reparations work: the continued prevalence of a reconciliation paradigm, white denial and lack of white participation, the need and yet difficulty of being very specific about reparations demands, the need for both grassroots and institutional buy-in, and that this work is so young and thus may not have "staying power" (236). Harvey presents a compelling case in the final chapters that reparations work has the capacity to overcome the impasses and shallowness that reconciliation work has created, and make significant material and structural changes that produce deeply meaningful and just interracial relationships along the journey.

Rare are those anti-racism discourses by white folks that engage history, structures and black voices that are seen as "radical" within most white spaces. The book's greatest strengths are that it addresses whiteness head-on and tells the undertold story of Black Power. Harvey's work is also refreshing in breaking through the echo chamber of reconciliation talk among white and even ethnic minority Christians. CCDA certainly falls within this audience. Though not unique in its critique and redundant at times, it might be one of the clearest and most succinct diagnoses of the inadequacies of the reconciliation paradigm. It is worth noting one critique Harvey anticipates from the reconciliation audience: that the book focuses too much on the white-black binary, making her study less relevant for other racial groups and perspectives. Harvey renders such a critique just as much of a failure as the reconciliation paradigm on which it depends.

One challenge for Harvey's reception is the book's lack of sustained biblical and theological language. This barrier may be another chance for whiteness to be masked *on biblical grounds*. Given that Harvey anticipates white denial and lack of participation as one of the greatest challenges to reparations work, it is disappointing that the book may be easily disregarded because of its lack of theological accessibility. The greatest shortcoming of Harvey's book may be its confidence in Black Power and reparations as the paradigm-shifter for future racial righteousness. I agree that the Church must have a paradigm shift away from reconciliation. And I'm thankful that white Christians and otherwise will be educated on Black Power. Yet, Harvey's interlocutors (within the footnotes and in-text) are almost exclusively first generation black liberation theologians, with virtually no mention of second and third generations. The book is underdeveloped in its articulation of the complexity within black religious thought, race theory and African American political philosophy. Will Harvey's focus on Black Power actually reinforce whiteness? To be determined. Still, I highly recommend this book as an important corrective to many racial missteps by the Church, especially white Christians.

PHOTOGRAPHY

from Then to Now

BY RACHEL GRACK

SEQUENCE

AMICUS | AMICUS INK

Sequence is published by Amicus and Amicus Ink
P.O. Box 227, Mankato, MN 56002
www.amicuspublishing.us

Library of Congress Cataloging-in-Publication Data
Names: Koestler-Grack, Rachel A., 1973- author.
Title: Photography from then to now / by Rachel Grack.
Description: Mankato : Amicus, 2022. | Series: Sequence | Includes bibliographical references and index. | Audience: Ages 7-10 | Audience: Grades 2-3 | Summary: "Full-color photographs and a running timeline illustrate important developments in the history of photography Topics feature camera obscuras, daguerreotypes and other early plate photography, film, lens design, digital cameras, and 3-D images. A table of contents, glossary, further resources, and an index are included"-- Provided by publisher.
Identifiers: LCCN 2019036298 (print) | LCCN 2019036299 (ebook) | ISBN 9781681519630 (library binding) | ISBN 9781681526102 (paperback) | ISBN 9781645490487 (pdf)
Subjects: LCSH: Photography--History--Juvenile literature. | Cameras--History--Juvenile literature.
Classification: LCC TR149 .K565 2022 (print) | LCC TR149 (ebook) | DDC 771.3--dc23
LC record available at https://lccn.loc.gov/2019036298
LC ebook record available at https://lccn.loc.gov/2019036299

Editor: Gillia Olson
Designer: Aubrey Harper
Photo Researcher: Bridget Prehn

Photo Credits: Alamy / age fotostock 26-27, Alistair Scott 19 (camera inset), Everett Collection Inc. 20-21, GL Archive 8, Howard Barlow 11, PRISMA ARCHIVO 7, Science History Images 10; Bellus3D 28; British Library / William Henry Fox Talbot 12-13 (all); Flikr / Collection of National Media Museum / Kodak Museum 15 (all), diser55 21 (inset), Nesster 23; Getty / Bettmann 4, Bloomberg cover; iStock / KOHb circuit texture (throughout); Leica Image Bank 19; Shutterstock / aquatarkus 24; Wikimedia / Anne Jea 16 (top), Evan-Amos 19 (film inset), Institut Lumière 16-17 (middle and background), Janke 16 (inset), Joseph Nicéphore Niépce/College of Liberal Arts Office of Information Technology, University of Minnesota 6-7 (background and inset), Westlicht Photography Museum in Vienna, Austria 9